8,95

Who Is This Christ?

GOSPEL CHRISTOLOGY AND
CONTEMPORARY FAITH

REGINALD H. FULLER

PHEME PERKINS

FORTRESS PRESS
PHILADELPHIA

Second printing 1984

Library of Congress Cataloging in Publication Data

Fuller, Reginald Horace.
  Who is this Christ?

   Bibliography: p.00
   Includes index.
   1. Jesus Christ—History of doctrines—Early church,
ca. 30-600—Addresses, essays, lectures. 2. Bible.
N.T. Gospels—Criticism, interpretation, etc.—
Addresses, essays, lectures. 3. Jesus Christ—Person
and offices—Addresses, essays, lectures. I. Perkins,
Pheme. II. Title.
BT198.F93 1983   232   82-48590
ISBN 0-8006-1706-1

1474I84   Printed in the United States of America   1-1706

Contents

Preface

In June 1980 the authors were invited to deliver some lectures on the christology of the gospels and contemporary faith at the Biblical Institute held at Trinity College, Burlington, Vermont. Our lectures were well received and appeared to mesh so well together that we thought it worthwhile to shape them into a jointly authored book. Since we come from such different backgrounds, this was a particularly attractive project. One of us is approaching the end of his theological career, the other is in the early stages of hers. One of us is an English Anglican (an Episcopalian), the other an American Roman Catholic.

There are some differences in our views, of course, and there are differences in our style and approach, but we hope that these differences will appear to be complementary rather than contradictory.

The division of labor in the ensuing chapters follows that of the lectures as they were given at Trinity College. Chapters 1, 4, 7, 9, and 10 are by Reginald H. Fuller; chapters 2, 5, 6, 8, 11, and 12 are by Pheme Perkins. Chapter 3 was written by Reginald Fuller from the tapes of a panel discussion in which we both took part.

We are happy to dedicate this book to Sister Miriam Ward, whose idea it was that we share the lecture series and under whose auspices it was delivered.

The Feast of the Epiphany 1982   Reginald H. Fuller
                                            Pheme Perkins

Abbreviations

AB	Anchor Bible
ATANT	Abhandlungen zur Theologie des Alten und Neuen Testaments
ATR	*Anglican Theological Review*
BFCT	Beiträge zur Förderung christlicher Theologie
BR	*Biblical Research*
CBQ	*Catholic Biblical Quarterly*
FRLANT	Forschungen zur Religion und Literatur des Alten und Neuen Testaments
HeyJ	*Heythrop Journal*
HDR	Harvard Dissertations in Religion
HNTC	Harper's New Testament Commentaries
HTR	*Harvard Theological Review*
Int	*Interpretation*
JBL	*Journal of Biblical Literature*
JSNT	*Journal for the Study of the New Testament*
JTS	*Journal of Theological Studies*
NovT	*Novum Testamentum*
NTS	*New Testament Studies*
NRT	*La nouvelle revue théologique*
RB	*Revue biblique*
SBLDS	Society of Biblical Literature Dissertation Series
SBS	Stuttgarter Bibelstudien
SBT	Studies in Biblical Theology
SHAW.PH	Sitzungsberichte der Heidelberger Akademie der Wissenschaften—Philosophisch–historische Klasse
SNTSMS	Society for New Testament Studies Monograph Series
VC	*Vigiliae Christianae*

1

Christology: Its Nature
and Methods

Christology as Response

The word "christology" is made up of two Greek words, *chris-tos* and *logos*. *Christos* literally means the "anointed one." This word in turn is a translation of a Hebrew word, *mešiah* (messiah). In fact, *Christos* would have been puzzling to a first-century Greek, and it is not surprising that it soon was mistaken for a proper name, and indeed became such even in ordinary Christian usage. Sometimes, too, it was confused with a better-known name, *Chrēstos*. The point is, however, that the roots of the first part of the word "christology" are found in biblical thought and Hebrew usage. The second part of the term, *logos*, is thoroughly Greek. Its simplest meaning is "word," the spoken word. From this it develops into a term for that which is expressed in speech, that is, human thought, reason. The root *log-* gives rise to the compound *-logia*, denoting "the science of." So already in Plato we get the word theo-logia,[1] literally "God-talk." Later, in dogmatic theology the term "christology" became one of the *loci* or topics of theological reflection. The term is also used by church historians, who speak of the "christological controversies" of the early church and of the "christological definitions," such as those of Nicaea and Chalcedon. All these expressions refer to human reflection on the person of Christ, particularly reflection about his divinity and his humanity and how both can be present in one person. But the very fact that christology conceals a combination of two very different ideas, one of them Hebraic, denoting appointment for a particular role in (salvation) history, and the other a Greek word, denoting reflection and ratiocination,

1

suggests something of a paradox. We must not exaggerate the difference between Hebraic and Greek thought, but there is a difference, for example, between Aristotle's *Metaphysics* and the book of Deuteronomy![2]

Systematic theology has normally treated christology (the doctrine of the person of Christ) before it has gone on to soteriology (the doctrine of the work of Christ).[3] It seemed logical to deal with who Jesus was, before dealing with what he did, for what he was determined what he did, or so it seemed. Yet our word "christology" reminds us that *Christos* is prior to *logia*, the phenomenon prior to reflection on it. In the order of human experience the "Jesus phenomenon" (to borrow a useful term of Edward Schillebeeckx's) came before reflection on it.

This has not always been obvious; indeed, it was not grasped until the later phases of biblical criticism. Christian orthodoxy, Eastern and Western, Catholic and Protestant alike, has in practice taken its basic material for christological reflection from the Gospel of John. There Jesus is represented as preaching, as his primary message, his own person—as contrasted with the Gospels of Matthew, Mark, and Luke—where the primary burden of his message is the kingdom of God. As long as the Fourth Gospel was thought to have been written by John the Beloved Disciple and the product of an eyewitness, it was easy to think that Jesus taught his disciples the true understanding of his person and that this christological teaching was therefore part of the Jesus phenomenon, part of the revelation brought by Jesus, rather than reflection on it. The critical view of the Fourth Gospel has shattered all that. The Fourth Gospel is now seen as the product of decades of reflection on the Jesus phenomenon, and that reflection has been allowed to color the whole presentation. While today we would not deny that the Fourth Gospel does enshrine some primitive and even authentic traditions, it is to the synoptic gospels—Matthew, Mark, and Luke—that we primarily have to look if we are to reconstruct the Jesus phenomenon. I say "reconstruct," because in the synoptic gospels too we have a problem. Although not so completely impregnated with christological reflection as the Fourth Gospel, the synoptic gospels also are colored by later reflection. Or, better, the authentic traditions—

sayings and memories of Jesus—have been constantly reapplied to new situations in the Christian community between its establishment after Easter and the composition of the synoptic gospels in their final form.

It is therefore generally agreed by critical scholars today that Jesus did not inculcate a christological interpretation of his person. Rather, to use Rudolf Bultmann's categories, he proclaimed the nearness of God's eschatological reign, enunciated the radical demand of God, and in his teaching and activity confronted men and women with a God who was at once far and yet near.[4] We would probably be correct in asserting with Günther Bornkamm that this activity evoked "messianic hopes and fears." We need not suppose that reflection on the significance of Jesus began only after Easter. Men and women already reflected on who he was and what his significance was. Some of them concluded that Jesus was the agent of Beelzebub, the prince of the devils. Some, like the high priest, feared that he might turn out to be the Messiah. Something like this must have come up when Jesus was investigated before the sanhedrin, otherwise he would not have been crucified as a messianic pretender—even if we grant, as we must, that the trial scenes before the sanhedrin, as we now have them, have been colored by the messianic faith of the post-Easter community. Jesus' friends, however, hoped that he would be the one to redeem Israel. Even if the Emmaus story of Luke 24 depends a great deal on Luke's artistry, the evangelist seems to have captured accurately the mood of the disciples after the debacle of Good Friday.[5] We are not told what kind of redemption they were thinking of, and we can hardly expect them to have spelled it all out for themselves as Paul was to do later on. At least some of the early disciples were nurtured on "anawim piety" (the piety of the "poor") and thought of God intervening to liberate the spiritually oppressed. Others may have cherished some kind of Zealotlike hope, even to the extent of looking for political deliverance from Rome—whether they embraced the Zealot program of violence or not.[6] If there is any historical basis to the story of Peter's confession at Caesarea Philippi (Mark 8:27–30), and if it is not purely a post-Easter creation,[7] Peter must have fostered some such hope before Easter. The point we are making is that any estimate and

interpretation of Jesus is by its very nature a *response*. Pre-Easter
christology, if there was any as we think there was, must have
been highly rudimentary, always inadequate, and sometimes erroneous. But it was never part of the original package. Jesus
talked about God and what God was doing and going to do and
what he demanded, and so brought his contemporaries face-to-
face with God's immediate presence. Only indirectly and by implication did this involve any claim about himself, his own person. If he believed that God was speaking in his own message and
active in his own deeds, this said something primarily about God.
That it had implications about Jesus himself came out from time
to time: "Blessed is he who takes no offense at *me*," (Matt. 11:6
par.) and "If it is by the finger of God that *I* cast out demons, then
the kingdom of God has come upon you" (Luke 11:20; cf. Matt.
12:28). But these are challenges to see God at work in Jesus, not a
claim to anything on his own part. Thus the original package, that
is, Jesus' message and activity, contains a "theology of Jesus";
the genitive is both subjective and objective, subjective in that it
is a declaration about God made by Jesus, and objective in that it
is a claim that God was uniquely speaking and acting in Jesus. But
Jesus left it to his contemporaries to draw their own conclusions
about who he was.

The Nature of the Response

In formulating their response, Jesus' contemporaries drew
upon the language of their own cultural traditions. Those reared
in *"anawim* piety"—the piety of the poor—naturally interpreted
him in *anawim* terms; those who had a Zealotlike background
conceived of him accordingly.[8] Tradition means the accumulated
experience of the past, in which people are nurtured and which
they bring to bear on new experiences, interpreting them along
similar lines. This does not mean that in interpreting Jesus they
were forcing him into the mold of their previous experience. All
new experiences, when really new, modify our understanding of
previous experience. Nowhere is this more true than in the case of
the experience of Jesus (objective genitive). By using terminology
from their own previous experience and hopes—for example, that
Jesus was the Savior of the *anawim* (see the infancy narratives in

Matthew and Luke), or that he was a quasi-Zealot messiah (see Mark's episode of Peter at Caesarea Philippi)—the early disciples were not defining Jesus. He remains the "one who fits no formula," as Eduard Schweizer has put it; he bursts the existing formulas when they are applied to him.[9] It would be claiming too much to suggest, as an earlier generation of scholars did, that Jesus deliberately and consistently reinterpreted existing titles such as Son of God, Son of Man, Messiah, Lord, and so forth. But when these titles were conferred on him (I leave open for present purposes whether Jesus actually used "Son of Man" as a self-designation), particularly after Easter, they were shattered and remolded by what he was and by what he had achieved. We cannot understand who he is by simply studying the pre-Christian meanings of the various titles. Not that such study is irrelevant, for their previous meanings do say something about the meaning of Jesus, or they would never have been used for him. But since these titles were shattered and remolded, they have to be understood in the light of the impact the Jesus phenomenon has had upon them.

Enough has been said to show where we stand in the debate between Rudolf Bultmann and Karl Barth as to which comes first, christology or soteriology, the person or the work of Jesus. In order of experience, there can be no doubt that soteriology comes first, however much in subsequent reflection we may be led in the end to speak, as dogmatics and systematics have done, of christology before soteriology. Perhaps it is really a question of which comes first, the chicken or the egg.

Christology: From Below or from Above?

The question about the right order of doing things—christology first, or soteriology—was largely a Protestant one. In recent years an analogous debate has taken place within Roman Catholic theology: whether christology should be done "from above" or "from below."[10]

Christology "from above" is the traditional *modus operandi*. One started with Christ as the eternal Son of God and second person of the Trinity and moved from there to his incarnation and earthly life, then (if one got that far) to his death, resurrection, and exaltation. Such a procedure has a *prima facie* justification in the christological hymns in the Pauline corpus and especially in the structure of John's Gospel, where the prologue (John 1:1–18) precedes the history. Christology from below begins with the history of Jesus, and then works back to the question of his preexistence and incarnation. The disadvantages of the former procedure and the advantages of the latter are plain to the modern critical scholar. But on the level of popular piety, christology from above is the normal procedure, and a christology from below seems threatening to faith.

What disadvantages does the critical scholar see in a christology from above? It tends toward docetism, apollinarianism, or monophysitism. In other words, it does violence to Jesus' humanity in order to preserve his divinity at all costs. It has all the answers about Jesus' history before the questions are asked. It is prepared to explain or explain away anything that suggests that Jesus had the limitations of a first-century Palestinian Jew. Jesus attributed the Pentateuch (Genesis–Deuteronomy) to Moses, Psalm 110 to David, the book of Jonah to sober history. Modern scholarship has more sophisticated ideas about the various authorships and regards Jonah as a didactic legend. But the fundamentalist says that either modern scholarship is wrong or Jesus was deliberately accommodating himself to the limitations of his own day (the right-wing form of the kenotic theory), or that he deliberately abandoned some divine attributes such as omniscience while keeping others when he became incarnate (the left-wing kenotic theory). So the disadvantage of christology from above is that it does violence to the history of Jesus. Indeed, in the final analysis it is unorthodox, because it is purchased at the cost of diminishing his full humanity (hence its docetist, apollinarian, or monophysitic tendencies). Moreover, its agreement with the christological hymns of the Pauline corpus and the structure of the Fourth Gospel is apparent rather than real. The preexistence element in the pre-Pauline hymns[11] is featured not for its own sake but in order to draw out the significance of the historical Jesus phenomenon. Those who composed or appropriated the hymns did so because they wanted to say something about that phenomenon, rather than because they wanted to speculate about a divine being prior to that history. As for the prologue of the Fourth Gospel, it is widely thought today that it was added at one of the later stages in the composition of the Gospel, either by the evangelist to the original narrative Gospel or by the final redactor to the composition of the evangelist. Therefore, the movement of Johannine christology was actually *from* below *to* above, *from* the historical Jesus phenomenon *to* its prior background in eternity. Hence in the order of development of Christian reflection, the below came first, and the above followed later. From below to above is the only acceptable way of doing New Testament christology. Only so can we avoid the temptation of manipulating the below to square with the above, or of raising problems with the below that are not there unless we are trying to conform our expectations of the "below" to our conceptions of its origin in the "above." We must therefore continually refer our "above" statements back to their primary source, to the Jesus phenomenon as experienced by the earliest disciples and the New Testament church. Presumably this is what the post-New Testament church of the patristic age thought it was doing. But often, in the christological debates that took place up to and beyond Chalcedon, one gets the impression that theologians occasionally forgot that they were talking about Jesus of Nazareth and instead were talking about abstractions like divinity and humanity, person, nature, hypostasis, hypostatic union, and so forth. And when, as in the *Tome* of Leo the Great, there was an attempt to hide this metaphysical christology from above in the below of Jesus' history, the effect was often to impose the metaphysics on the history and distort it.

Yet the problem is not really quite so simple. If we immerse ourselves first in the study of the Jesus phenomenon as such, we will find ourselves confronted in the first instance with a christology from below. But as we penetrate further, we shall find ourselves being led—cautiously, perhaps, at the start—to an "above" way of thinking, for in this historical Jesus, in his words and works, we find ourselves confronted with the claim that here is the presence of God himself. Hence there is already an "above" element in the Jesus phenomenon itself. This "above" element however, is in the first instance God himself, uniquely, definitively, and finally. It is not, to begin with, Jesus in his own being who is "from above." At its earliest stages, both before and, as we hope to show, later—after the Easter event—what we call christology is at this time really a "theology of Jesus." That is to say, the God present in Jesus is God himself. It is not that Jesus in his own being is identical with the God who is present in him. Of course this is not a "low" christology, even if the title "eschatological prophet" is used to characterize the Jesus thus conceived, for this is the unique, final, definitive—in short, eschatological—presence of God in a human being. Such a presence was never in a human being before, nor has it been since, nor—unless the eschatological quality of that experience of Jesus be completely negated—will there ever be until the end of time. But still, this is not to say that the God encountered in Jesus is Jesus himself. Some scholars today would be content with such a christology. We have to admit its attractions, and to say that it is all right as far as it goes, for that is as far as the church had come by about the year 50 C.E. Only with the Johannine literature do we really reach an "above" christology that is related to the actual being of Jesus himself rather than to God in the human being Jesus. Therefore, we must always remember that in the early days the movement of christology was from "below" to "above." It is particularly important for systematic theologians to remember this, even if they have their own reasons of logic for reversing the procedure and proceeding from above to below. They must always be aware of what they are doing and constantly refer back to the original order of apprehension. Otherwise they will find themselves in the same kind of problem that characterized the period of the greatest christological controversies and definitions: abstraction and latent docetism, apollinarianism, and monophytism.

Functional Versus Ontological Christology

We have already touched on the distinction between functional christology and ontological christology in connection with the alleged contrast between Hebraic and Greek thought. The earliest christologies were conceived not so much in terms of who Jesus was but rather in terms of what God was doing with him and through him. If these christologies spoke, as they came predominantly to do after Easter, of who Jesus was, it was not the result of abstract reflection on his person and nature or even his divinity as such. Indeed, the term "divinity" hardly occurs in the New Testament, and if we do use it in discussing New Testament data (for instance, as John Knox used it[12]) we are using it primarily to denote the role that Jesus accomplished in salvation history rather than what he was in himself ontologically or metaphysically. We must with similar caution speak of Jesus' "humanity" when discussing New Testament texts. The New Testament presents Jesus as a man,[13] that is, a concrete figure in history; it does not indulge in abstract reflection on his humanity as such. It is commonly observed that the Epistle to the Hebrews emphasizes the humanity of Jesus as no other writing in the New Testament does.[14] This is correct, but Hebrews does this in terms of history, not in abstract speculation. It speaks about Jesus' temptation and his struggle in Gethsemane, which qualify him to "sympathize" with us in our human infirmity.[15] It thinks of Jesus' humanity in functional terms. It speaks of Jesus' role in salvation history, the nature of his mission. The New Testament, especially in its latest developments in the Fourth Gospel, does pose ontological problems, but it hardly makes ontological statements, except perhaps in the Johannine prologue.[16]

Should we therefore confine ourselves to functional statements when doing christology? Such is the conclusion of many biblical scholars, notably Oscar Cullmann.[17] This conclusion aggravates systematic theologians and has been one of the main causes of the rift between exegesis and systematic theology. This rift, however, is regrettable and unnecessary. Functional christology inevitably raises ontological problems, particularly when the early Christians reached the point of affirming, as John's Gospel affirms, that what was incarnated in Jesus was an aspect of the being of God himself, an aspect that was one with God yet distinct from him, and that this aspect of the being of God was united in Jesus in a truly human life. How do these aspects of the being of God relate to one another, and how can they be affirmed without compromising Israel's basic faith (which the church inherited) that God is one? And how, too, could that aspect of God be identified with the human being Jesus of Nazareth without compromising his true humanity? Functional christology led inevitably in the New Testament to ontic statements, which in turn posed ontological problems. These problems had to be answered, not just for speculation's sake or out of intellectual curiosity, but in order to understand, live out, and proclaim the gospel of God's act of salvation in Jesus of Nazareth. We cannot set the clock back christologically and return to a purely functional christology, but this does not mean that we are committed in perpetuity simply to repeat the ontology of Nicaea and Chalcedon. We have to find the ontological language that will communicate in our day what the christological definition communicated in their day. That is a task of no small order, given that there is no universally accepted ontology today, as there was in the post-Constantinian age. The solution is not to abandon the task or to revert to a pure biblicism, but to persist in the search in our endeavor to answer meaningfully for our day what the church fathers were seeking to answer in their day.

Summary

We have sought to define christology as human reflection and response to the "Jesus phenomenon," which we have in turn defined as the historical appearance of Jesus and his aftereffect in the Easter experience of the first disciples. These definitions are in agreement with a modern critical understanding of the Gospels, according to which the earthly Jesus proclaimed the kingdom of God rather than himself, and himself only obliquely and indirectly as the point where the kingdom of God was breaking through into human history.

In making this response, the Christians of the New Testament era—like their successors—drew on the images and concepts of their own cultural tradition. In the process, these images and concepts received decisive correctives: Their meaning was shaped by the Jesus phenomenon rather than by their own prior experiences. Yet those experiences played a part in conditioning their response to the phenomenon, and therefore the study of the prehistory of their images and concepts is indispensable to the subject.

We then distinguished between two basic types of christology: christology "from below" and christology "from above," and functional christology and ontological christology. We saw that the "from below" and the functional type preceded the other type, the "from above" and ontological. New Testament scholars work mostly with the first type; systematicians with the second. It is an impediment to the sound development of theology and therefore of the church's faith and life that these two types should be considered antithetical. Each type has its place and role. Only the priority of the "from below" and functional type must always be maintained, and the christology of the second type must never lose sight of the fact that it is subsequent reflection on the problems posed by the first type. Otherwise systematic theology will become abstract and divorced from the reality and experience to which it was a response. This is what happened, or threatened to happen, during the period of the great christological controversies and the christological definitions. Exegetical study of the New Testament christologies can therefore serve to give life and reality to the church's christological confession today, rather than undermine it.

FOR FURTHER READING

Hengel, M. *Jews, Greeks, and Barbarians: Aspects of the Hellenization of Judaism in the Pre-Christian Period.* Eng. trans. John Bowden. Philadelphia: Fortress Press; London: SCM Press, 1980. One of several works demonstrating how recent studies of Palestinian Judaism have revealed the deep inroads made by Greek culture in Palestine itself after Alexander the Great.

Rahner, K. *Theological Investigations.* Volume 17. Eng. trans. M. Kohl. New York: Crossroad; London: Darton, Longman & Todd, 1981. Pages 24–38 present the two ways of doing christology, "from above" and "from below."

Rahner, K., and Thüsing, W. *A New Christology.* New York: Seabury Press, 1980. A New Testament exegete and a systematic theologian combine to produce a modern christology starting "from below."

Knox, J. *The Humanity and Divinity of Christ.* Cambridge: At the University Press, 1967. A noted New Testament scholar ventures into the systematic field. He traces the steps by which christology developed, and then interprets that history and its theological significance.

Fitzmyer, J. A. "Nouveau Testament et christologie: Questions actu-
elles," *NRT* 103 (1981): 18–47; 187–221. A Roman Catholic scholar
gives a question-and-answer summary of the results of New Testament
exegesis with regard to the various aspects of Jesus' life that have a
bearing on christology.

NOTES

1. Plato *Republic* 379A.

2. Recent studies of Palestinian Judaism have revealed the deep inroads made by Greek culture in Palestine itself after Alexander the
Great. See M. Hengel, *Jews, Greeks, and Barbarians* (Philadelphia: Fortress Press; London: SCM Press, 1980).

3. For the argument between Karl Barth and Rudolf Bultmann on this
question, see K. Barth, "Rudolf Bultmann: An Attempt to Understand
Him," in *Kerygma and Myth*, ed. H. W. Bartsch (London: SPCK, 1972),
2:96. Barth asserts that soteriology, while part and parcel of christology,
"is nevertheless secondary to it and precedes it."

4. R. Bultmann, *Jesus and the Word* (New York: Charles Scribner's
Sons, 1958), chaps. 2, 3, and 4.

5. G. Bornkamm, *Jesus of Nazareth* (New York: Harper & Row,
1960), p. 172.

6. For an interpretation of Jesus in Zealot terms, see S. G. F. Bran-
don, *Jesus and the Zealots: A Study of the Political Factor in Primitive
Christianity* (Manchester, Eng.: Manchester University Press, 1967).
For a more balanced view on the question, see M. Hengel, *Was Jesus a
Revolutionist?* (Philadelphia: Fortress Press, Facet Books, 1971).

7. See my traditio-critical analysis of Mark 8:27–33: R. H. Fuller, *The
Foundations of New Testament Christology* (New York: Charles Scribner's
Sons; London: Lutterworth Press, 1965), pp. 109–11.

8. For a characterization of *"anawim* piety," see R. E. Brown, *The
Birth of the Messiah* (New York: Doubleday & Co., 1977), pp. 350–55.

9. E. Schweizer, *Jesus* (Richmond: John Knox Press, 1971), pp.
13–51, uses this expression as the title of his second chapter.

10. The most succinct description of the two types of christology, that
"from below" and that "from above," will be found in K. Rahner, "Die
zwei Grundtypen der Christologie," in *Schriften zur Theologie* (Ein-
siedeln: Benziger & Co., 1972), pp. 227–38. Cf. idem, "Christology Today?" in *Theological Investigations* (New York: Crossroad; London: Darton, Longman & Todd, 1981), 17:24–38.

11. For a discussion of these hymns, see below, Chapter 5, pp.
58–63.

12. J. Knox, *The Humanity and Divinity of Christ* (Cambridge: At the
University Press, 1967).

13. The New Testament usually speaks of Jesus as *anthrōpos* generically, and it is this word that carries christological freight (e.g., Rom. 5:12–19; 1 Cor. 15:21, 45–47) in connection with Paul's Adam christology. In three Lukan passages where *anēr* is used, there is no stress on Jesus' being male; instead, it is a term used in connection with an eschatological prophet christology (Luke 23:50; 24:4; Acts 2:22).

14. See, e.g., J. A. T. Robinson, *The Human Face of God* (Philadelphia: Westminster Press; London: SCM Press, 1973), pp. 155–61.

15. Heb. 2:18; 4:15; 5:7–9.

16. O. Cullmann, *The Christology of the New Testament* (Philadelphia: Westminster Press, 1959), p. 3.

17. Ibid., p. 4.

2

The Historical Jesus
and Christology

Reflecting on the Significance
of Jesus

Christology begins when people come to reflect on the great testimonies to faith in Jesus. What is the implication of that faith embodied in poetic and symbolic statements? What conclusions do we draw from that primary language of religious experience about God, the world, ourselves? Though no theological system can exhaust the religious witness of our faith, we cannot live without the understanding that the theologian brings to the tradition. The compactness and multiple reference of symbols make them the starting point for as many false or misleading interpretations as for true or helpful ones. The centuries of struggle and controversy over the appropriate interpretation of the person and work of Jesus attest to this difficulty. Christians claim that what God accomplished in Jesus was for the salvation of all humanity in every place and time. As peoples and times change, we must find new ways to express the truth about Jesus, so that those peoples hear that truth as "gospel" for them. This process of reflection began with the first apostles. They had to explain their conviction that Jesus was the expected Messiah both to fellow Jews and then to the increasing number of Gentiles who joined the movement. The process continues whenever Christians try to explain why people should find in Jesus God's revelation of the way to salvation, to the resolution of the root problem of human life through the reconciliation of God and humanity in Jesus.

However, the quest to articulate who Jesus is must acknowledge the complexity of the very sources on which we draw to answer the question about Jesus. We speak of the fundamental conviction of christology as Jesus is God's revelation or, in an even more striking formulation, God is Jesuslike.[1] How then do we find out about this Jesus? None of the gospels provides a biography of Jesus or a verbatim record of his teaching. Each has a different portrait of Jesus, which is already an interpretation of his significance for particular Christians in particular places. Of course, these portraits are not antithetical. Their presence in the canon of Christian Scripture suggests that each has been found to be a faith-full portrait of Jesus by the believing community.

Some argue that christology does not have to ask any questions beyond what is presented in these four portraits. Theologians do not have to use the various methods of analysis to reconstruct an image of the "historical Jesus" which would have given rise to the later testimony about him. They argue that human language and culture evolve by reinterpreting great figures for each age in ways that are quite unhistorical. The more important a person has been in the history of a people, the less his or her image corresponds to any norm of historical accuracy. Those of us trained as historians frequently groan loudly at mass media presentations of people and events we have spent a lifetime trying to understand. The settings, actions, words, and characterizations of those people all betray the preoccupations of twentieth-century North Americans. Yet some would argue that such "filtering" is the only way in which the great figures of the past continue to speak in the present. Perceived in the modern idiom, they live on by sponsoring new insight and action even if those insights and actions might not be traced to anything such people could be expected to have intended within their own context. Such approaches to christology focus on the story of Jesus as a symbol that opens up new possibilities of life for people. They frequently read that story in the psychological categories which have come to dominate the twentieth-century Western perception of what it means to be human.

One influential approach is framed in the categories of evolution of consciousness. It looks to religious myths and stories as manifestations of the fundamental structures of human consciousness. The great religious leaders like Buddha, Jesus, or Mohammed are seen to embody a depth of consciousness that the believer must seek to attain. Often such approaches assume that the great religious traditions coincide in their understanding of mystic awareness of the divine. Thus, in this approach, spiritual and not historical insight is required in order to verify the authentic transformation of human consciousness from the mundane, limited, egocentric perspective to the universal compassion characteristic of the divine.

A purely historical approach to the question of Jesus may expose particularities that separate us from earlier times and cultures. The biblical tradition continues to develop through the historical mediation of language from the earliest traditions of Israel down to the believing communities of the present. That past is also part of the community's present at each stage in its life. The commitment to reshaping the religious, symbolic, and institutional forms of the "great cultures" of the ancient Near East has been mediated through the biblical tradition to our own culture.[2] Just as one can be too wedded to the distance established by history, so one can be too ahistorical. Is it really true that religious consciousness transcends the particularities of culture, a unique religious symbolism, or a particular understanding of the divine? Paul found himself at odds with the Corinthians over such a question. He did not agree that Christianity was an expression of an individualized Wisdom (Sophia) mysticism. Instead, he insisted that Christian formation of consciousness is possible only within the community in which charity, dictated by the need of the weakest members, is the norm for religious faithfulness. That norm cannot be set aside by human spiritual achievements—even those of the apostles themselves.[3]

The Death and Resurrection of Jesus as the Focus of Salvation History

Another approach to the problem of christology stems from the early kerygma itself. Our earliest evidence of Christian preaching (kerygma) begins with the proclamation that the death and resurrection of Jesus was God's reconciliation of a sinful people with himself. It stands as God's final answer to the long history of human disobedience.[4] Jesus' death and resurrection "for us" represents God's unconditional "yes" to humanity. At the same time, it embodies a renewed call to that humanity to turn and receive the life, grace, and spirit made possible for those who believe. The pressing question in these formulations is "What is God's salvation?" The question of who Jesus is cannot be separated from the question of salvation. Twentieth-century theologians must try to explain the significance of the death/resurrection of Christ within the parameters set by our own questions about salvation.[5] Our questions include concern with historical movements of human liberation; the quest for psychological healing; and the need for global responsibility for resources and environment.

The attempt to formulate the significance of salvation in Jesus for such questions will inevitably require the effort to go behind the words of Scripture to the experience of salvation at which they point. For example, Rudolf Bultmann argued against supposing that the biblical language about reward was meant to help people calculate their salvation. Rather, it is symbolic language that points to the seriousness of our choices about how we live our lives: "The motive of reward is only a primitive expression for the idea that in what a man does his own real being is at stake—that self which he not already is, but is to become."[6] Other theologians object to the attempt to express the meaning of the biblical message in terms borrowed from existential philosophy, because that philosophy plays to a fundamental weakness of the Western understanding of self. The twentieth-century West has invested too much in the individual as the center and norm of all action.[7] This false emphasis has left people handicapped by lack of adequate language and symbols for the problems we face in our emerging global community. The Bible always addresses the people of God primarily, and the individual secondarily as a member of that community. Its language may provide the needed corrective to our symbolic poverty if its message of salvation is presented in global rather than individualist terms. That message can be seen as one of global justice,[8] of solidarity with the perspective of the suffering rather than that of the powerful,[9] or of care for all creation.[10] Unless our christology can speak in these larger contexts, it will remain a reflection of that retreat into subjectivism which has been typical of Christian theology for the past two centuries.[11]

Resurrection is seen as the key that unlocks the significance of Jesus. It points to him as the expression of God's will for the salvation of all people and for the renewal of creation. But Jesus is more than a symbol for salvation which comes from God to his creation. The Jesus who is preached as having died and been raised is also remembered as a particular person. His particular fate, crucifixion, is remembered in the proclamation of his death and resurrection. That particular mode of death carries with it further implications. It suggests that his message and activity must also be bound up with his place in salvation history. Jesus is not a purely symbolic person who could as well be replaced by some universal symbol, term, mode of religious consciousness, or the like. Instead, the kerygma implies that the teaching, aims, and fate of a very particular individual belong to the salvation of a humanity estranged from God.

The Historical Jesus and Christology

Without this anchor in the message and life of Jesus, christology could rapidly recreate Jesus in the image of a specific culture or ideology. The universality of the gospel requires that we express the significance of Jesus differently in different times and places. It does not expect that such new formulations will embrace the perceptions of human life and the solutions to its problems worked out by particular cultures without question. This distinction presumes, of course, that humans are capable of self-transcendence, that they can overcome their immediate cultural situation and can appropriate symbols and experiences which are not part of that setting. Without such a presupposition, we could hardly claim to be guided by any revelation beyond that of our immediate consciousness, let alone claim to find the foundation for our faith in Scripture.

The past century has seen a flood of new information about antiquity in the fields of archaeology, classics, and history and of information about nontechnological cultures more like those of biblical times in anthropology and sociology. Biblical exegetes search both the methods and the results of such studies for further insight into the biblical writings, their times, their cultural surroundings, and their historical background. At the same time, we recognize that all attempts to reconstruct the biblical world depend on hypothesis, on historical intuition, and even on imagination to suggest what meanings particular words and actions held for those who heard or participated in them. We may even find that we do not have a clear idea of the meaning of particular words or expressions in the Bible, since we lack adequate parallels to the biblical expressions. We may be forced to make an educated guess based on parallels remote in time from the text with which we are concerned. The expression "Son of man" is an example of a phrase whose meaning is not clearly defined. Consequently, there is little agreement among scholars about what the expression means when applied to Jesus.

Honesty about the limits of our methods and knowledge should never be used as an excuse to sell short the positive accomplishments of those methods. Some hypotheses, such as the claim that Jesus was an advocate of revolutionary violence, simply will not stand the test of historical credibility. On the other hand, no historian can deny that Jesus' execution by death on a cross raises the question "Just or unjust?" Further, the involvement of some Jewish religious authorities in the events leading to the death of Jesus suggests that Jesus' message or actions must have raised some challenge to the religious status quo. He was perceived not as a slightly demented peasant from Galilee but as someone against whom public action had to be taken. Thus, even before the content of Jesus' message has been specified, the facts of his death show that a decision about Jesus' guilt or innocence implied a decision about serious public issues. No reconstruction of the ministry of Jesus can be adequate to our sources if it does not attempt to suggest what those issues were.

The kerygma also points to the fact that after Jesus' execution a group of his followers begin to proclaim that he "is raised" or "is exalted to the right hand of God." Such a claim goes beyond the assertion that Jesus was innocent of the religious and/or legal charges brought at his trial. It applies the most exalted language available for the fate of a righteous human being to the destiny of Jesus. That same perception of his destiny includes an awareness that they, his disciples, are now charged with the messianic task of gathering the people. Thus, the development of symbols for

Jesus to express his messianic significance, language we identify as explicitly christological, begins along with the birth of a community conscious of its special place in salvation history. Christology is born along with a new gathering of the people of God. This development calls for a further judgment about Jesus, that is, a judgment about what he might have intended to set in motion. Of course, the historian can only describe the questions called forth by the events that surround the life and death of Jesus. Historical analysis cannot compel the assent of faith, which sees in these events God's universal plan of salvation.[12]

No study of the historical Jesus would fail to locate the focus of his message and action in his message about God. Sometimes that focus is taken to imply that later Christians deserted Jesus' preaching when they began to formulate explicit claims about him. Most theologians argue, however, that one cannot understand Jesus' preaching without recognizing that from the start his preaching implied a relationship with God and an insight into God's purposes that challenged the established religious leadership. Since Jesus' authority was not legitimated by the usual social categories,[13] those who became his disciples had found it necessary to make some decision about the nature of Jesus' relationship with God. None of the normal patterns quite fit. Jesus could not be a priest, since he did not come from a priestly family. He was not quite a prophet in the Old Testament sense, as his teaching is not delivered as "word of the Lord" standing over against the people in judgment. He is not quite an apocalyptic preacher, since he does not teach esoteric interpretations of the signs of the end, thunder against the wicked, and proclaim God's judgment upon them. Instead, he speaks of a presence of the rule of God and conducts a ministry that seeks out sinners. He is certainly not a teacher who teaches his disciples how to interpret the Law in scribal or Pharisaic fashion. Instead, he castigates such interpretations as departures from God's intent in the Law. Though he speaks in parables and proverbs, he is not a teacher of wisdom, for he does not present these insights as guidance for the young amid the follies of human life.[14] Instead, his parables often contain surprising twists in human action. They reverse the cynicism of the world by insisting that people can and do live in the presence of God's rule.[15] Some may have heard that he was a wandering miracle worker. Yet he seems to have insisted that those miracles were really signs that God's power is alive and well in the world, quite capable of overthrowing Satan.

The image of perplexed fascination and hesitant messianic expectation which all the gospels present as the initial response to Jesus would be appropriate to such teaching and action. Jesus seems to have deliberately associated his ministry with the rule of God. He addressed God as *Abba*, "father," an Old Testament expression for the relationship between God and his people, and he taught his disciples to do the same. In so doing, he claimed that God is taking up a new intimacy with his people. To some, that way of speaking may have seemed to violate the proprieties of religious language, which insisted that the holy name of God never be pronounced even in reading Scripture. His association with sinners and outcasts appears to have been carried to the point of including them in table-fellowship meals symbolic of the gathering of the righteous in the new age. Both actions are highlighted by contrast with the rules for holiness among the Essenes. They excluded from the meal any members of the sect who had violated rules of holiness by which the community lived. Their rule book, *The Manual of Discipline*, includes penalties for anyone who pronounces the divine name or behaves with disrespect for the community, the Law, or a fellow Essene. At the same time, the Essenes felt that God's spirit, poured out on the community, enabled them to live a life of such obedience. The extreme seriousness with which the Essenes took these points of religious practice helps us appreciate the shocking character of much of Jesus' behavior. It violated fundamental symbols for the holiness of the people, purity and separation from all that is sinful.

We have no reason to suppose that Jesus himself was caught up in the euphoria that sometimes accompanies the breaking of old boundaries in the name of religious reform, though perhaps the disciples were. Two sayings about Jesus' death have a strong claim to authenticity, since they are not developed in light of later events as the other passion predictions: Luke 13:32–33 and Mark 14:25. They both suggest that at the very least Jesus saw himself to be running the risk of suffering or dying as a result of his identification with God's cause. He could have taken the fate of John the Baptist as a warning for his disciples, though all the gospels present the disciples as unable to grasp the suffering of Jesus until after the resurrection. Even if we cannot be sure that Jesus claimed that his death would have soteriological significance, as some scholars think,[16] his acceptance of suffering as part of his mission on God's behalf is of crucial importance to later claims about the death of Jesus. The biblical God suffers with, even through, his people. He does not manipulate them as pawns in a cosmic chess game. He does not condone the "slaughter bench of history," even when its suffering may have led a wayward people to repent. Consequently, as New Testament traditions recognize almost from the beginning,[17] only the obedient suffering of the righteous can represent God's love toward his people.

The affirmation about Jesus' approach to suffering and death implied in those announcements about his fate cannot be established irrefutably by historical analysis alone. Nonetheless, such analysis may suggest that the person who makes such an affirmation of faith has a plausible reason for doing so. Jesus' vision of God's presence with his people and his impending action on their behalf was not disconfirmed by the suffering and rejection he experienced at the hands of some of the righteous, those who would have been expected to be most receptive to God's messianic salvation.[18] This rejection emphasizes the paradoxical character of God's rule as it is embodied in the teaching, the actions, and finally the death of Jesus, whose cause is identified with that rule. The rule of God does not force its presence on humanity with great wars of messianic conquest or with the dramatic conversion of all Israel and then the Gentiles. Instead, God continues to be represented in the world by what appears weak and insignificant. Thus, when christology comes to reflect on the divinity of Jesus, it is properly concerned with Jesus as God's image in the world. Jesus is not to be identified with the God-concept of Judaism or of one of the other religious or philosophical movements of the time. Rather, Jesus must be allowed to qualify any God-concept so that it is adequate to the revelation of God that emerges in Jesus.[19] Nor should such a concept be merely a symbolic extension of the cross. The place of the historical person Jesus in the kerygma suggests that the Christian God-concept must also embrace the God who emerges in the preaching of Jesus.[20]

Summary

Christology faces the challenge of speaking about Jesus' significance in a way that the message can be heard in different cultures and at different times. Consequently, theologians are always sensitive to the varieties of symbolic language, cultural patterns, and even expectations of salvation. A genuinely biblical faith cannot embrace either a radical ahistoricism that would locate faith in some timeless religious consciousness, or a radical cultural relativization that would reduce all contact with the past to "what it says to us." The center of the kerygma appears in the affirmation that God and humanity are reconciled in the death and resurrection of Jesus. At the same time, the people of God, the object of God's loving concern, is set on a new path that will lead it beyond the confines of Judaism to identification with all humanity.

The Jesus of whom this affirmation is made is not stripped of his historical particularity. He is not a symbol or a representative human who could as easily have been replaced by anyone else. Consequently, the question about his teaching and ministry is not irrelevant to christology. Of course, historical inquiry is a limited endeavor of probabilities and hypotheses linking its evidence together in intelligible patterns. It will not provide irrefutable proofs for the claims that Christian faith makes about Jesus. Nor, given the nature of our sources, can it come close to providing a picture of Jesus and his mission so detailed that all historians will agree with it. Rather, we make probable presentations of the teaching and ministry of Jesus. We make suggestions about the impact of his teaching on the various audiences that heard him.

The broad lines of agreement in such presentations provide a framework that should be reflected in any account of Jesus' significance. Any presentation of Jesus and his ministry will have to account for the public character of his death. It will have to suggest an explanation for the convergence of religious and political authority in his execution. Since the hypothesis that Jesus was a Zealot is quite unlikely, the issue of his religious views and his following seems to be the one around which such an explanation

will be formed. Further, both his teachings and his actions
suggest a ministry that sought to identify with God's rule in a way
that stood quite outside the usual patterns of legitimation. Therefore, the question of Jesus' identity, role, or relationship to the
divine forced itself on those who came in contact with him. Either
he was blasphemous, a fool, or he spoke with divine authority.
Modern interpreters often use the image of "eschatological
prophet" or "suffering servant" as the best approximations to the
self Jesus presents in his ministry. Yet none of the conventional
categories seem adequate. Jesus' use of *Abba* and his table fellowship extend the claims that he makes about the presence and
the rule of God into important areas of religious action: how one
addresses God and how one symbolizes the eschatological community of the righteous. He challenges conventional behavior on
both fronts. Finally, Jesus appears to have anticipated that his
ministry would entail suffering and rejection. He would not receive the universal acclaim one might expect for God's Messiah.
This anticipation suggests that Jesus' fate, too, belongs to the
cause of God's rule, the cause with which Jesus is identified.
Thus, the question about God is at stake in the question about
Jesus from the beginning. One cannot speak about the significance of Jesus without making claims about God and his relationship to humanity as it is revealed in Jesus.

FOR FURTHER READING

Brown, R. E. "Who Do Men Say That I Am?—A Survey of Modern
Scholarship on Gospel Christology." In *Biblical Reflections on Crises
Facing the Church*, pp. 20–37. New York: Paulist Press, 1975.
Provides an overview of the approaches to christology and biblical
scholarship.
Keck, L. *A Future for the Historical Jesus*. Philadelphia: Fortress Press,
1980, reprint ed. Reissue, with an epilogue, of a 1971 work assessing
recent developments in Roman Catholic circles. Keck's lucid discussion of the theological significance of the quest of the historical Jesus
provides an important corrective to studies that rely simply on
sayings-traditions deemed authentic. He points out that such a limited
base does not provide an adequate image of the saving vision of God
that is represented in Jesus.
Perrin, N. *Rediscovering the Teaching of Jesus*. New York: Harper &

Row, 1967. A classic example of the methods and criteria used to determine authentic teachings of Jesus. The concluding chapter traces the history of the question about the relevance of knowledge about the historical Jesus for the faith of Christians.

Robinson, J. M., and Koester, H. *Trajectories Through Early Christianity.* Philadelphia: Fortress Press, 1971. Pages 158–231. In these two chapters, Koester asks whether the diverse christological perspectives embodied in the different traditions about Jesus can be harmonized. He suggests that the death/resurrection creed became normative because it takes human life and suffering seriously enough to enable Christianity to become a church and not a sect.

Kasper, W. *Jesus the Christ.* Eng. trans. V. Green. New York: Paulist Press; London: Burns & Oates, 1976. Kasper combines the picture of Jesus gained from historical Jesus research with a contemporary philosophical hermeneutic about the meaning of salvation. The New Testament perspective is to be articulated in light of modern insights into anthropology, society, and the role of mediating structures in human self-consciousness. Jesus' identification of himself with God's cause forms the basis of christological assertions about Jesus. Inevitably, such a systematic appropriation of New Testament materials harmonizes the different christological perspectives embodied in the Jesus traditions.

Perrin, N. *Jesus and the Language of the Kingdom: Symbol and Metaphor in New Testament Interpretation.* Philadelphia: Fortress Press, 1976. Perrin's later work, much influenced by the hermeneutics of symbols, recognizes that an adequate representation of Jesus' message about the Kingdom must come from an understanding of symbolic language. Conceptual statements will not grasp the transformation of reality made possible through the use of tensive religious symbols.

Van Beeck, F. J. *Christ Proclaimed: Christology as Rhetoric.* New York: Paulist Press, 1979. Pages 30–149. Van Beeck describes the importance of symbolic language and rhetoric in understanding the whole history of christology. He suggests that the rhetoric of worship and witness which flows from the resurrection evaluates all the human concerns we bring to christology.

Thompson, W. A. *Christ and Consciousness: Exploring Christ's Contribution to Human Consciousness.* New York: Paulist Press, 1977. Thompson approaches the issue of christology from the viewpoint of the development of human consciousness. The problem of the divinity of Christ is set in relationship to the development of a language to probe the expansion of human consciousness made possible through Christ.

———. *Jesus, Lord and Savior: A Theopathic Christology and Soteriology.* New York: Paulist Press, 1980. Thompson turns to the quest of the historical Jesus within the perspective of the development of consciousness. Christology must proceed from the fundamental insight that God is "Jesuslike." Consequently, what is known about Jesus is fundamental to a Christian understanding of God.

NOTES

1. See the discussion of the Christian God-concept in W. A. Thompson, *Jesus, Lord and Savior* (New York: Paulist Press, 1980) pp. 113–15.

2. See H. Schneidau, *Sacred Discontent: The Bible and Western Tradition* (Berkeley and Los Angeles: University of California Press, 1977).

3. See the provocative articles by R. A. Horsley, "Spiritual Marriage with Sophia," *VC* 33 (1979): 30–54; and "Consciousness and Freedom Among the Corinthians: 1 Corinthians 8–10," *CBQ* 40 (1978): 574–89.

4. See S. K. Williams, *Jesus' Death as Saving Event*, HDR 2 (Missoula, Mont.: Scholars Press, 1975), and the discussion of reconciliation in Paul by J. A. Fitzmyer, "Reconciliation in Pauline Theology," in *To Advance the Gospel* (New York: Crossroad, 1981), pp. 162–85. See also R. P. Martin, *Reconciliation: A Study of Paul's Theology* (Atlanta: John Knox Press, 1980).

5. See the appropriate remarks of E. Schillebeeckx, *Jesus: An Experiment in Christology*, Eng. trans. H. Hoskins (New York: Seabury Press, 1979), pp. 597–638.

6. R. Bultmann, *Theology of the New Testament* (New York: Charles Scribner's Sons, 1951), 1:15.

7. See the objections to the contemporary privatizing of religious experience and the adoption of "religion as fulfillment" in M. Marty, *The Public Church* (New York: Crossroad, 1981), pp. 23–43.

8. See J. Moltmann, *The Crucified God* (New York: Harper & Row, 1974), pp. 145–92.

9. See J. Metz, *Faith in History and Society* (New York: Seabury Press, 1980), pp. 73–132.

10. See B. Wicker, *The Story-shaped World: Fiction and Metaphysics* (Notre Dame, Ind.: Notre Dame University Press, 1975), pp. 59–69.

11. See the objections to the Christocentrism of modern theology by E. TeSelle, *Christ in Context: Divine Purpose and Human Possibility* (Philadelphia: Fortress Press, 1975), pp. 127–46.

12. Schillebeeckx, *Jesus*, pp. 44–87, 604–42.

13. See the discussion of charismatic figures in the time of Jesus in H. C. Kee, *Christian Origins in Sociological Perspective* (Philadelphia: Westminster Press, 1980), pp. 53–73.

14. See C. E. Carlston, "Proverbs, Maxims, and the Historical Jesus," *JBL* 99 (1980): 87–105; and my discussion of wisdom traditions and the parables: Pheme Perkins, *Hearing the Parables of Jesus* (New York: Paulist Press, 1981), pp. 35–45.

15. Perkins, *Hearing the Parables of Jesus*, pp. 15–33.

16. See Thompson, *Jesus, Lord and Savior*, pp. 70–71, and M. Hengel, *The Atonement: The Origins of the Doctrine in the New Testament* (Philadelphia: Fortress Press, 1981), pp. 71–72, for the argument that Jesus attributed a soteriological significance to his death.

17. They seem to have been at least partially dependent on traditions that had developed around the Maccabean martyrs; see the extensive discussion in Williams, *Jesus' Death as Saving Event*.

18. Paul's pained reflection on the fate of Israel in Rom. 9–11 shows that the question of the Jewish "no" to Jesus continued to plague Christians.

19. See Thompson, *Jesus*, pp. 113–61.

20. See my discussion of God in Jesus' parables: Perkins, *Hearing the Parables of Jesus*, pp. 90–110, 178–96.

3

The Easter Event

The Relevance of the Resurrection
to Christology

At first it might seem surprising that a book on christology should include a whole chapter on the resurrection of Jesus. There are two reasons for this, the immediate and practical one being that this book is in some measure a reaction to Edward Schillebeeckx's first volume on christology, the work entitled *Jesus: An Experiment in Christology*. In this book he includes two large sections on the subject of the resurrection: first, from a historical viewpoint[1] and second from a christological[2] viewpoint. Since Schillebeeckx's treatment of the Easter event has proven highly controversial (in fact, was one of the points that got him into trouble with the Curia), it seemed necessary to clarify our own position on the matter. The second is that the Easter event as such is the presupposition of all New Testament christology.

There are no less than four areas where Schillebeeckx's *historical reconstruction* of the Easter event raises problems.

The first of these areas (in the order raised by Schillebeeckx himself), though hardly the first in order of importance, concerns the empty tomb and its relation to the resurrection tradition.

Second, and more important, is Schillebeeckx's treatment of the primitive kerygmatic formulas that deal with the resurrection, particularly 1 Cor. 15:3–8.

Third, there is his suggestion that the primary Easter experience of the first disciples was one of conversion and forgiveness, and that in order to verbalize their experience the disciples availed themselves of an established model in Judaism, the conversion story, in order to narrate them.

Fourth, there is the question of the final and unrepeatable

character of the resurrection appearances and how they relate to subsequent appearances of the Risen One and to other kinds of spiritual experiences that occurred in the early Christian communities.

Is *the empty tomb* indispensable to resurrection faith? Many scholars regard it not only as secondary but also as irrelevant to that faith. This is often expressed in the remark "If the bones of Jesus of Nazareth were discovered lying somewhere in Palestine, we could still believe in the resurrection." Then there are groups of scholars in the United States,[3] in Britain,[4] and in Germany[5] who take it as axiomatic that the empty tomb story is a "late legend." The main reason for this widely held opinion is that Paul is completely silent about the empty tomb, even in 1 Corinthians 15, and that the story first appears in the relatively late Gospel of Mark, that is, not earlier than ca. 70 C.E. The first appearance of a tradition in a written document does not necessarily mean that that tradition originated at the time of its composition. In the case of Mark 16:6–8 there is every indication that the tradition it enshrines has undergone successive adaptations before it reached its finally redacted form in Mark and that it is therefore much older. It is impossible to say when the earliest nucleus of the tradition originated, but I have argued elsewhere that it began with a report of Mary Magdalene to the disciples on their return from Galilee after the first resurrection appearances, informing them that she (and probably other women) had found Jesus' tomb empty.[6] There is a surprising amount of evidence that there was a tradition about a message conveyed by Mary Magdalene to the disciples.[7] It has multiple attestations and may therefore be accounted as primitive tradition. We cannot at this date verify the accuracy of Mary's report; all we know is that the disciples accepted it as compatible with their vision of the Resurrected One.

Those who argue for the lateness of the empty-tomb tradition generally regard Mark as the origin of all the other traditions, so that it has but a single attestation. Matthew and John, however, may have had access to a common non-Markan source for the appearance to Mary Magdalene by the (empty) grave site, and in any case John is widely held to be independent of the synoptists.[8] Luke 24:1–12 is usually thought to be dependent on Mark 16:1–8, and the summary in Luke 24:22–23 is generally taken to be purely redactional. It may, however, contain nonredactional traditional but non-Markan elements belonging to the cycle of non-Markan traditions behind both Luke and John.[9] Such multiple attestation would be further support for the primitive origin of the empty-tomb tradition. But again, this does not prove its historicity.

Schillebeeckx locates the origin of the empty-tomb tradition in an annual local cultic observance at the graveside on Easter Sunday.[10] He makes much of the fact that the empty-tomb story speaks not of the "third day," like the kerygma, but of the "first day of the week." This, he argues, points to the nonkerygmatic origin of the tradition.[11] The problem with this theory is that there is no historical evidence for a cult focused on the sacred rites at Jerusalem until the post-Constantinian era. In a celebrated treatment of this topic, Gregory Dix argued that the eschatological perspective of the early church precluded both a concern for past historical commemorations and curiosity about the sacred rites. Such concerns did not arise, he thinks, until the slackening of eschatological tension.[12] In any case, it is probable that the early Jerusalem community was quartodeciman, that is, it observed the paschal feast on the Jewish date, 14–15 Nisan, rather than on the following Sunday.[13] I would therefore abide by my earlier view that the empty tomb pericope was the conclusion of the Passover haggadah and that the motivation behind its inclusion was to lead to the Easter proclamation "He is risen!"[14]

Let us now revert to the question of whether the discovery of Jesus' bones in Palestine would make any difference to Easter faith. People often ask about the nature of the resurrected body. The answer is, we do not know. It is not fair to say that if some remains were discovered which we could be sure were the bones of Jesus it would make no difference to our concept of the resurrection. The early church adopted the apocalyptic view (one of several current Jewish views) that the resurrection body was a *transformation* of the physical body. On that view one would probably not expect to find bones. On the other hand, if we turn the question around, an empty tomb does not of itself prove a thing. The best it could prove is that someone must have robbed the grave. So affirming the resurrection must be independent of finding an empty tomb. Such a discovery would leave one puzzled and distressed, and afraid that the tomb had been robbed—elements we actually find in the accounts of Matthew and John.

We turn now to our second topic, namely, *the primitive kerygmatic formulas* in which the resurrection was proclaimed. It is surprising that Schillebeeckx did not deal with 1 Corinthians 15 *before* discussing the empty tomb, as most exegetes do today,[15] for it is here, rather than with any of the narratives at the ends of the four gospels, that the quest for the earliest resurrection traditions must start. Indeed, 1 Cor. 15:3–8 is probably one of the two most primitive of the traditions in the New Testament, the other being the Pauline account of the institution of the Eucharist. We have in 1 Cor. 15:3–8 a pre-Pauline formula with some Pauline redactional additions. The words translated in the Revised Standard Version as "delivered" and "received" are technical terms indicating the handing on of earlier traditions. Paul must have "received" them prior to around 50 C.E. when he "delivered" them to the Corinthians. The mention of Cephas and James as recipients of appearances, and the fact that Paul met with both these men on his first postconversion visit to Jerusalem in around 35 C.E., takes us to within five years of the events described, and to second- and even first-hand witnesses (Cephas and James, Paul). Schillebeeckx takes the statement "he appeared" as originating not in primary witness but in subsequent theological reflection on a prior experience, namely, the experience of conversion/forgiveness.[16] We shall discuss conversion and forgiveness and their place in the Easter traditions below. Now Paul uses the word "appeared" with reference to his own Damascus experience, and he was a firsthand witness. He was not articulating some other experience which lay behind this expression. We cannot get back behind the statement "he appeared" to something more primary. "He was raised" is an inference, but a primary inference deduced from "he appeared," interpreted as revelation (cf. Gal. 1:15–16, "reveal his Son to me"), not a secondary inference from a primary experience of conversion and forgiveness.

Let us look at this formula in depth. The first statement is about the death of Christ, which is said to have occurred "in accordance with the scriptures." Here we do have reflection, but very early reflection. Today we would not want to press the notion that the Old Testament predicted Jesus' death in so many words. What it did (especially in the Psalms) was set forth the pattern of the righteous sufferer, humiliated and abandoned by God.[17] Jesus fit into this pattern in a quite final way. Next comes mention of the burial, but nothing about the empty tomb. What is important is that Jesus really died. The statement "he was buried" looks *back* to the death rather than *forward* to the resurrection. Dead and buried—*finis*! Upon that the resurrection bursts as an incredible, unprecedented *novum*, as the eschatological event par excellence. Here we must enter a caveat. The formula says "was raised," not that Jesus raised himself as though he had one last miracle in his pocket; like his death, it was "in accordance with the scriptures." The picture of the vindication of the righteous sufferer, like the picture of his God-forsakenness, was adumbrated in the Old Testament and fulfilled in Jesus.

Further, "was raised" is to be distinguished from resuscitation or, as Schillebeeckx's translator puts it, "reanimation." It is not that Jesus returned to the same mode of existence that was his prior to death, but rather that he was translated into a wholly new mode of existence. Paul discusses this later in 1 Corinthians 15 in relation to the resurrection of the believers, and Phil. 3:21 shows that he conceived of Jesus' resurrection in the same way.

The passage 1 Cor. 15:3–8 does not specify the exaltation, but presumes it. Other primitive formulas (e.g., Phil. 2:6–11) do specify the exaltation, but not the resurrection. One, however, always implies the other, and as Schillebeeckx correctly observes, "resurrection is the *terminus a quo* and exaltation the *terminus ad quem* of the same event."[18] The same thing is true of the "rapture model" by which Luke especially articulates the Easter event. This too presumes the resurrection. Resurrection is the primary, but not the only, model by which the first witnesses articulated their revelatory experience.

Our third area of concern is Schillebeeckx's choice—as the primary model of Easter narrative—of what he calls *the conversion model* in preference to the Pauline model of resurrection appearance-mission. He claims that there was a Jewish conversion model on the basis of some passages from Isaiah and from the

Testament literature.[19] There appears to be insufficient evidence for postulating such a narrative type or for the hypothesis that the resurrection appearance stories were developed after such a model. It is curious that there is no footnote indicating the secondary source from which Schillebeeckx derived this theory.[20] What he fails to notice is that in the history of the tradition the simple listing of appearances precedes the appearance stories, and therefore the stories seem rather to be the result of expanding the bald statement "he appeared to . . ." into narrative form. If there is any Old Testament or Jewish model for this, it would seem to be that of the theophany or angelophany rather than conversion story, as the Greek word *ōphthē* (he appeared) indicates.

But Schillebeeckx does make an important point when he observes that the experience of conversion or forgiveness is integral to many of the postresurrection appearances. Peter in John 21 is clearly forgiven for his denial of Jesus. And the saying in Luke 22:32—"when you have turned again"—interprets what will happen to Peter later as a conversion. The rest of the Twelve had likewise forsaken Jesus and scattered, and therefore their reassembling and the appearance to them involved an offer of forgiveness, even if it is not explicitly mentioned. In the case of the Twelve, we do have a charge to proclaim forgiveness to others, thereby implying that they themselves have received forgiveness. James the brother of the Lord had not followed the earthly Jesus, and therefore the appearance to him involved a conversion to faith. How this element of forgiveness or conversion entered into the experience of the five hundred and more brethren and of "all the apostles" is impossible to make out. But Paul relates his apostolic call quite specifically to his previous activity of persecuting the followers of Jesus and speaks of that call as a preeminent act of grace, a notion close to forgiveness (1 Cor. 15:9–10). Schillebeeckx, however, is methodologically wrong in basing so much in the conversion stories on the book of Acts for the interpretation of the appearances stories.[21] These are not primary materials for the interpretation of Paul's Damascus road experience, but largely the product of Lukan theology. In fact, it is widely held among exegetes today that the author of Luke-Acts has downgraded what Paul understood to be an apostolic call to the level of a conversion.[22] If there is any conversion model, as Schillebeeckx claims, its influence would seem to have entered only at a comparatively late stage in the development of the tradition, with the author of Luke-Acts. Prior to that, the conversion or forgiveness element is a secondary effect of the Easter experiences, not their constitutive element. That element is revelatory and christological (Gal. 1:12).

The fourth and final concern is *whether the resurrection appearances are final and unrepeatable* and *how they relate to subsequent visions of the risen Christ* such as those of Stephen (Acts 7:55), of Paul himself (2 Cor. 12:1–5), and of John the seer (Rev. 1:9–16). Paul is most instructive at this point, since he was the recipient both of a postresurrection appearance and of subsequent visions. It is clear that he differentiates sharply between the two. The appearance on the Damascus road was given to him "last of all." Therefore he cannot regard his subsequent visions as repetitions of his Easter experience. Both are visionary in character, and as psychological phenomena it would be difficult to distinguish between them. Rather, it is their function in salvation history that differentiates them. The Easter experiences are concerned with the foundation of the church and the inauguration of its mission. The subsequent visions serve in one way or another the ongoing life of the church. Whatever their similarities or differences from a purely psychological point of view, the Easter appearances belong to the *eph' hapax*, the once-for-all character of the Christ event.

Was the Resurrection Real for Jesus?

There is a final question to which any book on christology today must address itself. A number of radical scholars have recently denied the reality of the resurrection as an event involving Jesus in his own person. Such a position was already anticipated by some of the older liberals. I remember many years ago challenging the late E. W. Barnes, Bishop of Birmingham and author of *The Rise of Christianity*,[23] as to whether he accepted the statement "Jesus was raised from the dead." His answer was that the influence of all great men continues after their deaths and that this is as true of Jesus as it was of Socrates! Rudolf Bultmann, whose theol-

ogy of the Word was very different from the liberal Protestantism
of Bishop Barnes, once accepted the statement "Jesus rose into
the kerygma" as an adequate expression of what he understood by
the resurrection.[24] A variant of this interpretation is found in
Willi Marxsen's now well-known statement that the resurrection
means *"Die Sache Jesu geht weiter"*—what Jesus stood for continues after his death.[25] Schillebeeckx is at pains to distinguish
his position from that of Marxsen,[26] but at times he seems to
equate the statement "God raised Jesus from the dead" with the
statement that the offer of salvation made in Jesus' earthly life is
renewed after Easter. In his Bampton Lectures, the late Geoffrey
Lampe proposed a christology of the Spirit.[27] According to this,
the man Jesus was the definitive presence of God's Spirit (=
God's presence and activity in the world and in humanity). But he
has neither pre- nor post-existence. It is not Jesus who personally
lives after death, but the Spirit that was in him. Henceforth the
Spirit of God is the "Spirit of Jesus." God acts from now on toward us always with reference to the Christ event. The Holy
Spirit's work henceforth involves a constant renewal of the revelation and redemption wrought in Jesus of Nazareth in the ongoing
life of the church and of the world. Since so many of the christological titles accorded to Jesus in the New Testament referred
originally to the Resurrected One, and since postexistence was
asserted of Jesus from Easter on, it is important to reach a decision on this issue if we are to present both a New Testament
christology and a christology for today.

All these interpretations—that of Schillebeeckx included—
seem to take the statement "God raised Jesus" or the term "resurrection" of Jesus to be an articulation of another, more basic experience. They may formulate this basic experience differently.
For Marxsen it was that the earthly Jesus is experienced after Easter as still evoking faith. Schillebeeckx defines the basic experience as one of conversion—in other words, the disciples are restored to faith in Jesus. Lampe, in turn, defines the basic Easter
experience as an experience of the Spirit of God, a Spirit who is
henceforth the Spirit of Jesus.

But what is the basic experience of Easter? The fundamental
tradition in 1 Cor. 15:3–8 (which we have argued is not the prod-

uct of subsequent reflection on the primary experience but the testimony of first- and second-hand witnesses to the experience itself) is an *ōphthē* (appearance) experience, an experience of encounter with Jesus as resurrected. Now all that the radical critics have claimed to be the reality of Easter—that Jesus rose into the kerygma, that the cause of Jesus continues, that faith in Jesus as God's eschatological deed is renewed after the debacle of Good Friday, that God's offer of salvation is renewed, that the Spirit is henceforth the Spirit of Jesus—is profoundly true. But they are the *effects* of God's raising Jesus from the dead, the effects of Jesus' resurrection, not the resurrection itself. In other words, the Easter event is primarily what God did with Jesus, not something that God did primarily with the disciples. What he did with the disciples was only secondary. We can readily admit that the language of "resurrection" is derived from Jewish apocalyptic and is therefore in itself mythological. But it is mythological language for something that God did with Jesus, not just for what God did with the disciples. If we want nonmythological language to describe what God did with Jesus at Easter, the best we can do is say that God translated Jesus into eschatological existence, into life out of death. Hence Jesus' postexistence must be retained as one of the primary data for New Testament christology.

There is a second reason, also vitally connected with New Testament christology, why it is important to retain Christ's postexistence. For Paul, Jesus' resurrection is closely connected with Jesus' status as Second Adam. As such, he is raised to be the first fruits of those who have fallen asleep (1 Cor. 15:20). His resurrection is not only chronologically prior to but also christologically determinative of all other resurrections and of a renewed cosmos. As in Adam all die, so in Christ shall all be made alive. If Christ be not raised from the dead, the believers' own possibility of eschatological existence is undercut. It is therefore not surprising that Lampe was forced to make his eschatology a completely realized one to maintain that those elements of future eschatology which survive in the New Testament are simply hangovers from pre-Christian apocalyptic.[28] This, however, is not demythologizing the kerygma, it is elimination. For these reasons, therefore, the postexistence of Jesus is an integral part of the New Testament witness and part of the data for christology.

Summary

The Easter event is an essential part of the data for christology. Its nature must therefore be explored, and we chose initially to do this by an examination of four points raised by Schillebeeckx's treatment of the resurrection in his book *Jesus*: the status of the empty tomb narrative; the evaluation and interpretation of the primitive kerygmatic formulas, especially 1 Cor. 15:3–8; the theory that the primary Easter experience was one of forgiveness and conversion; and the final and unrepeatable character of the Easter experiences.

We argued that the empty-tomb narrative is shown by the long tradition history of Mark 16:1–8 and by multiple attestation to be rooted in a very early tradition, though it is impossible to demonstrate its historicity. We were unimpressed by the suggestion that the empty-tomb story originated in a cultic celebration at the tomb in Jerusalem. We preferred to see in it a tradition taken up into the Christian Passover haggadah.

The most primitive tradition we have of the Easter event is 1 Cor. 15:3–8. It says nothing of the empty tomb. It affirms Jesus' resurrection as an act of God. The appearances are to be understood as revelatory encounters in which God disclosed Jesus to the disciples as alive out of death.

The lists of appearances are not the result of subsequent reflection on a conversion or experience of forgiveness. Conversion and forgiveness are secondary effects of the appearance (*ōphthē*) experiences.

Paul differentiates clearly between his encounter with the risen Christ on the Damascus road and subsequent visions. Their difference is not ascertainably psychological but lies in their function in salvation history. They belong to the once-for-all (*eph' hapax*) of the Christ event, founding the community and inaugurating its mission.

Finally, we discussed whether the postexistence of Jesus is dispensable. We outlined briefly several radical proposals for eliminating Jesus' postexistence. We rejected these attempts on two grounds. First, we argued that the various alternative proposals equate the resurrection with its secondary effects. Second, the concept of resurrection, derived as it is from Jewish apocalyptic, needs to be demythologized; but this is to be done by interpreting it, not by eliminating it. We proposed as a demythologized interpretation that God translated Jesus after death into eschatological existence. Further, Jesus' resurrection is that of the Second Adam, that is, it is christologically determinative of the resurrection of the believers and of the apocalyptic renewal of the cosmos. As such it is integral to the New Testament message and therefore to christology.

FOR FURTHER READING

Schillebeeckx, E. *Jesus: An Experiment in Christology*. Eng. trans. H. Hoskins. New York: Seabury Press, 1979. Pages 320–97 deal with the Easter event historically, and pp. 518–32 deal with it theologically. The present chapter is largely a critique of those pages.

Perrin, N. *The Resurrection According to Matthew, Mark, and Luke*. Philadelphia: Fortress Press, 1977. Published after the author's regrettably early death. Perrin treats the Easter narratives from a redactional point of view, relating their theology to the overall theology of the respective evangelists.

Evans, C. F. *Resurrection and the New Testament*. SBT 2/12. London: SCM Press, 1970. This is one of the earliest of a spate of books to appear in the 1970s on the Easter narratives, and it is written by the most outstanding pupil of Sir Edwyn Hoskyns. It treats the resurrection from a historical and theological viewpoint, is somewhat skeptical in its treatment of the empty tomb, and holds that the appearance narratives are incapable of harmonization.

Marxsen, W. *The Resurrection of Jesus of Nazareth*. Eng. trans. M. Kohl. Philadelphia: Fortress Press; London: SCM Press, 1970. Marxsen is concerned with the objective character of the Easter event. It is not just the rise of faith in the redemptive significance of the cross (Rudolph Bultmann), but the event which caused the continuation of what Jesus stood for after the crucifixion. Like Bultmann, however, Marxsen cannot say what happened between God and Jesus. He traces the appearance tradition exclusively to Peter's experience and stresses Peter's reassembling of the Twelve.

Alsup, J. E. *The Post-Resurrection Appearance Stories of the Gospel Tradition*. London: SPCK, 1975. A doctoral dissertation written under the late Leonhard Goppelt. This is the most thorough history-of-tradition study of the appearance narrative available in English. After a careful critique of his predecessors, Alsup rejects any linkage of the appearance with apocalyptic visions and relates them instead to the Old Testament anthropomorphic theophanies.

Dhanis, E., ed. *Resurrexit: Actes du Symposium International sur la Résurrection de Jésus*. Vatican City: Liberia Editrice Vaticano, 1974. Papers from an international group of scholars which discuss all facets of the New Testament treatment of resurrection, followed by an extensive bibliography of writings on the resurrection from 1920 to 1973 and a briefer bibliography of materials from 1800 to 1919.

NOTES

1. E. Schillebeeckx, *Jesus: An Experiment in Christology*, Eng. trans. H. Hoskins (New York: Seabury Press, 1979), pp. 320–97. Schillebeeckx has replied to his earlier reviewers (of the original Dutch version) in idem, *Interim Report on the Books Jesus and Christ* (New York: Crossroad, 1981); on the resurrection and christology, see pp. 74–93. Although he now uses stronger language about Jesus' being alive, Schillebeeckx still adheres to the conversion model, does not distinguish between appearance lists and stories, and bases too much on Acts 9, 22, and 26.

2. Schillebeeckx, *Jesus*, pp. 518–71.

3. E.g., N. Perrin, *The Resurrection According to Matthew, Mark, and Luke* (Philadelphia: Fortress Press, 1977), p. 80.

4. E.g., C. F. Evans, *Resurrection and the New Testament*, SBT 2/12 (London: SCM Press, 1970), pp. 75–76; G. W. H. Lampe and D. M. MacKinnon, *The Resurrection: A Dialogue Between Two Cambridge Professors in a Secular Age* (London: Mowbray, 1966), pp. 18ff.

5. E.g., H. Grass, *Ostergeschehen und Osterberichte* (Göttingen: Vandenhoeck & Ruprecht, 1962), pp. 20–23.

6. R. H. Fuller, *The Formation of the Resurrection Narratives* (Philadelphia: Fortress Press, 1980), p. 56

7. See Mark 16:7; Luke 24:10–11, 22–23; and John 20:2. Matt. 28:8 may be only an inference from Mark.

8. P. Gardner-Smith, *Saint John and the Synoptic Gospels* (Cambridge: At the University Press, 1938), influenced a whole generation of Johannine studies (e.g., Bultmann, Dodd, R. E. Brown) in opting for John's independence of the synoptists. The tide has recently turned through the influence of Norman Perrin, who thought John was dependent on Mark. See his *The New Testament: An Introduction* (New York: Harcourt Brace Jovanovich, 1974), pp. 228–29. But Perrin's life was devoted to the study of Mark, and he never worked independently on John. See R. E. Fortna, "Jesus and Peter at the High Priest's House: A Test Case for the Question of the Relation Between Mark's and John's Gospels," *NTS* 24 (1978): 371–83 and the bibliography there.

9. For the usual redactional view of Luke 24:22–24, see R. J. Dillon, *Eye-witnesses and Ministers of the Word: Tradition and Redaction in Luke 24* (Rome: Pontifical Biblical Institute, 1978), pp. 108–10. For the pos-

sibility of a non-Markan origin of the Lukan redaction, see J. Jeremias, *Die Sprache des Lukasevangeliums* (Göttingen: Vandenhoeck & Ruprecht, 1980), and J. E. Alsup, *The Post-Resurrection Appearance Stories of the Gospel Tradition* (London: SPCK, 1975), pp. 114–16.

10. Schillebeeckx, *Jesus*, pp. 335–36. Schillebeeckx is here following B. van Iersel, "Jezus' verrijzenis in het Niewe Testament. Informatie of interpretie?" *Concilium* 6 (1970); 53–65, n. 10, esp. 57–60. Van Iersel, in turn, is following a line of scholars: Schillebeeckx (1955), Nauck (1957), Kremer (1968), Delorme (1969), Schenke (1969²).

11. Schillebeeckx, *Jesus*, p. 336.

12. G. Dix, *The Shape of the Liturgy* (London: Dacre Press, 1945), pp. 349–51.

13. B. Lohse, *Das Passafest der Quartadecimaner*, BFCT 2/54 (Gütersloh: Gerd Mohn, 1953).

14. R. H. Fuller, *The Formation of the Resurrection Narratives* (Philadelphia: Fortress Press, 1980), pp. 68–70.

15. Such is the approach, e.g., of J. Pfammater, X. Léon-Dufour, C. F. Evans, G. O'Collins, and J. F. Jansen.

16. Schillebeeckx, *Jesus*, pp. 380–85.

17. On the importance of the pattern of exaltation of the suffering righteous in first-century Judaism, see G. W. Nickelsburg, *Resurrection, Immortality, and Eternal Life in Intertestamental Judaism* (Cambridge, Mass.: Harvard University Press, 1972).

18. Schillebeeckx, *Jesus*, p. 534.

19. Ibid., p. 384.

20. Both bibliography and footnotes for ibid., pp. 380–85, are somewhat meager. In the panel, we tried to come up with the name of an exegete who gave Schillebeeckx the idea, and it was pointed out that the nearest footnote refers to "R. Fuller" (!).

21. Ibid., pp. 360–79.

22. G. Klein, *Die zwölf Apostel* (Göttingen: Vandenhoeck & Ruprecht, 1961), pp. 144–59.

23. E. W. Barnes, *The Rise of Christianity* (New York and London: Longmans, Green & Co., 1947), pp. 172–75.

24. For Bultmann's original treatment of the resurrection in his demythologizing essay, see Rudolf Bultmann, *Kerygma and Myth*, ed. H. W. Bartsch (London: SPCK, 1972), 1:38–42.

25. W. Marxsen, *The Resurrection of Jesus of Nazareth*, Eng. trans. M. Kohl (Philadelphia: Fortress Press; London: SCM Press, 1970), pp. 138–48.

26. Schillebeeckx, *Jesus*, p. 393.

27. G. W. H. Lampe, *God as Spirit*, The Bampton Lectures 1976 (Oxford: Clarendon Press, 1977).

28. Ibid., pp. 171–74.

4

The Titles of Jesus in Early Christology

The Significance of Easter for Christology

Christological response to Jesus began, however tentatively, inadequately, and even erroneously, during his earthly life. But it was after Easter, after his followers saw the resurrection to be God's vindication of Jesus and his cause, that an explicit christological assessment of Jesus was firmly established in the Christian community. The Proclaimer became the Proclaimed (Rudolf Bultmann). That was the effect of Easter. To many this has seemed like a "monstrous imposition" (George Bernard Shaw) on the simple message of Jesus. But today it is generally agreed, even in the Bultmann school, that there was a real continuity between the eschatological proclamation of the earthly Jesus and the christological proclamation of the post-Easter community. We may pinpoint two reasons for this. First, as we have seen, Jesus presented his own words, activity, and person as the decisive place where God's eschatological activity was to be discerned.[1] His person, though not the major burden of his proclamation, was often latent behind his words and deeds, and occasionally it surfaced: "Blessed is he who does not stumble at *me*" (au. trans. of Matt. 11:6 / / Luke 7:23). This we have called a theology of Jesus rather than a christology proper. Second, as we examine the so-called "two stage" christology of the post-Easter kerygma, the first stage, namely, the earthly life of Jesus, is presented precisely in terms of a "theology of Jesus":

> Jesus of Nazareth, a man attested to you by God with mighty works and wonders and signs which *God did through him* in your midst (Acts 2:22).

God anointed Jesus of Nazareth with the Holy Spirit and with power; . . . he went about doing good and healing all that were oppressed by the devil, for *God was with him* (Acts 10:38; cf. 2 Cor. 5:19).

The emphasis in the italicized phrases is not on who Jesus was in his earthly life but on what God was doing through him, just as it had been (in more oblique terms) in Jesus' own proclamation.

If we ask who and what Jesus was in this early kerygma, the answer, in phenomenological terms, would be a charismatic prophet and healer. God anointed him with the Holy Spirit (Acts 10:38), and he performed healings and exorcisms. However, the context in which all this is presented is that of eschatological fulfillment. God was present *uniquely and finally* in Jesus, not in the way in which he had been present in charismatic figures before him. We may say, then, that the effect of Easter initially on the assessment of the earthly Jesus is not to introduce a christology for the first time or, strictly speaking to begin with, an explication of a previously implicit christology as such, but rather a more confident and direct assertion of the same type of "theology of Jesus" which Jesus himself had held.

But after Easter the earliest Christian community did not content itself with the continuation of an explication of Jesus' assessment of his own earthly career. It went on to speak of a second phase of his activity. Jesus was now taken up into heaven, waiting to come again (Acts 3:21), or he was exalted and reigning at the right hand of God (Acts 2:33). God's eschatological, salvific action in Jesus did not cease with his death; the "theology of Jesus" continues after Jesus' death and becomes an explicit christology.

For the earthly stage of Jesus' career we soon find the application of the titles Servant (Acts 3:13, 26; 4:27, 30), Holy One and Righteous One (Acts 3:14), and implicitly through the application of the fulfillment citation Deut. 18:15 to Jesus, the (eschatological) prophet (Acts 3:22–23). These are all clearly titles denoting the role Jesus played in salvation history, the role of being the one in whom God was uniquely, definitively, and eschatologically active.

For the heavenly phase the titles used are *Christos* (Messiah), *Kyrios* (Lord; cf. Acts 2:36; Phil. 2:11), and Son of God (by applying Ps. 2:7 to Jesus at his resurrection; cf. Rom. 1:4).[2] It would be quite wrong to characterize such a christology as adoptionist, at least in the sense that term bore in later christological controversy. Such formulas are not saying that he became ontologically what he was not before—or, as a former colleague of mine once put it, that Jesus was "a man who graduated in divinity with honors." Rather, the formulas are saying that at his resurrection or exaltation Jesus embarked on a new role in salvation history. The former role, during his earthly career, was that of eschatological prophet, proclaiming the advent of God's eschatological reign. His new role as Christ, Lord, and Son of God is to direct the community and its mission from heaven and to be present in its proclamation and common life through the Spirit. Initially, therefore, it was found appropriate to apply to Jesus in his postexistence a new series of titles. But they, no less than the earthly set, are functional and salvation-historical in character. Nor does the restriction of these titles to Jesus' postexistence mean that only the second phase of his activity was accorded a christological assessment, for already the titles accorded his earthly existence were christological in character. We cannot deduce from this "adoptionist" christology, as William Wrede did, that the earthly life of Jesus was "unmessianic," unless the term "messianic" is pressed in its most literal way to mean the actual title "messiah."[3] The affirmation that God was active in him in a unique, definitive way during his earthly life, and that therefore he was Prophet, Servant, and the Holy and Righteous One, means in a broader sense his earthly life was in fact messianic and christological.

The Retrojection of the Titles
of Jesus

Raymond E. Brown has described the development of New Testament christology as a process of "retrojection," that is, the pushing back into the earthly life of christological titles that had originally been applied to Jesus' postresurrection activity.[4] We must avoid thinking of christological development in terms of a unilinear, uniform, and ubiquitous process.[5] More primitive christologies continued to survive alongside more developed ones even in the same communities (otherwise the evidence for them would not have survived in the New Testament documents).[6]

Perhaps the easiest title to retroject into the earthly life of Jesus was *Christos*, or Messiah. As we have seen, Jesus' friends and enemies alike proffered him that title, though in an erroneous or inadequate sense Jesus appears never to have unequivocally accepted it. And beyond all doubt he was crucified as a messianic pretender. Easter had demonstrated that he who had thus died was accepted and recognized by God as Messiah, though in a sense quite different from what his enemies had meant by that title at the crucifixion. At Easter, God vindicated Jesus, not as a Zealot leader but as the bringer of eschatological salvation. It was therefore an easy step to say that Jesus had died as *Christos*, as Messiah (1 Cor. 15:3). Strictly speaking such a title must have meant that Jesus died as Messiah, or *Christos* designate. As long as early Christians were thinking in terms of Acts 2:36 and held that God had enthroned Jesus as Messiah (*Christos*) they could hardly have thought otherwise. But then another step seems to have been taken. Already, as we have seen, Jesus was regarded as having been during his earthly life a charismatic prophet-healer. God has "anointed" *(chriō)* him with his Spirit (Acts 4:27; 10:38). In saying this the early Christians must have been thinking of Jesus' baptism, and it may be that Jesus himself interpreted his baptism as his prophetic anointing, even if he never spoke of his being anointed.[7] Hence, the title *Christos* (from *chriō*) would fittingly cover the whole of Jesus' ministry, his eschatological preaching, his exorcisms and healings, and above all his death. It is important to notice, however, that this retrojection of a title, originally applied in the full Christian sense to Jesus at his resurrection and exaltation into his earthly life, is not the christologizing of a life that was originally nonchristological. It means that the title *Christos* took over the functions of the earlier titles: Servant, Holy One, Righteous One, Prophet. Neither the self-understanding of Jesus nor the earliest post-Easter kerygma is falsified or altered by this retrojection. Moreover, the term *Christos* is still being used in its functional, salvation-historical sense. It does not imply that Jesus is now something other than he believed himself to have been during his actual earthly life, or other than what his disciples in the earliest post-Easter believed him to have been while still on earth. The constant element remains that God was acting definitively and salvifically in Jesus' earthly ministry. Retrojected into the earthly ministry, the title *Christos* still asserts a "theology of Jesus."

We do not know whether it is correct to speak of a retrojection of the title *Kyrios* into the ministry of Jesus. It is historically probable that Jesus was addressed as *Mar(i)* during his earthly life.[8] Initially, it would have been a title of respect, as when it was used of any ordinary rabbi. Gradually, however, it would come to mean more to the disciples as they were impressed by Jesus' unprecedented authority.[9] Jesus' execution as a criminal must have radically called into question the suitability of the title *Kyrios*. Easter, however, effectively restored it to him. God had made Jesus *Kyrios* in a sense far above that in which it had ever been predicated of him during his earthly ministry (Ps. 110:1). The way is now open for something of *Kyrios*'s post-Easter sense to be retrojected into the earthly ministry. It implied an authority which the resurrection had vindicated.

The situation with the title Son of God is far more complex. To begin with, it is important to distinguish, as Ferdinand Hahn has shown, between the Father/Son usage and the title Son of God.[10] The former has its origin in the earthly Jesus' use of *Abba*,[11] although there is no unimpeachable evidence that Jesus actually spoke of himself as the "Son" in any unique sense.[12] The title Son of God, on the other hand, is associated with *Christos*. It originates in the royal ideology of Israel and, as we have seen, was applied to Jesus from his resurrection under the influence of Ps. 2:7. There is fairly clear-cut evidence that Ps. 2:7 projected backward into the earthly life of Jesus to his baptism, to his transfiguration (it is unclear whether Son of God was first retrojected to the transfiguration and thence to baptism or vice versa), and finally to his conception/birth.[13] Taken by itself, this process would suggest a christologizing of what had been regarded previously as an unchristological life. However, traditio-historical analysis of the baptism and transfiguration stories lends support to the thesis that in an earlier stage of the tradition both pericopes were framed not in terms of a Son of God but in terms of a *pais*, or

servant, christology.[14] The voice from heaven may originally have
said, "You are my servant, my beloved" (cf. Isa. 42:1). This
would be the same christology of the earthly life as in the kerygma
of Acts 2, 3, and 10. Such a christology could have its roots in the
self-understanding of the historical Jesus, who as we have already
noted probably looked back on his baptism by John as his decisive
call to eschatological mission.[15] If this is how the baptism tradition developed, then the Son of God title in the baptismal voice
simply took over the functions of the earlier image of servant. The
process, once more, does not involve the christologizing of a nonchristological life.

The next development to note is the sending-of-the-Son pattern.[16] Bultmann and his disciples have supposed that the
sending-of-the-Son concept came into early Christianity through
a borrowing of the Gnostic redeemer myth.[17] This thesis, which
originates in the history-of-religions school, is generally regarded
today as discredited.[18] However, it is still often assumed that the
sending-of-the-Son concept is derived from Jewish wisdom speculation and therefore presupposes the Son's preexistence.[19] It is
true that the sending-of-the-Son formulas occur in writers who
otherwise hold a preexistence christology, namely, Paul, Hebrews, and John. It should be noted, however, that there is a
difference between the sending schema and that of the preexistence hymns. In those hymns the Preexistent One becomes incarnate on his own initiative, whereas in the sending-of-the-Son pattern it is God who takes initiative in sending his Son.[20] Again, the
sending-of-the-Son idea occurs in one instance that is totally innocent of preexistence christology, namely, in the synoptic parable of the wicked husbandman (Mark 12:1–12 // Matt. 21:33–46
and Luke 20:9–19). That parable, even if it does not go back to
the historical Jesus, or at least does not go back to him in its present allegorized form, is certainly pre-Markan and either earlier
than, or contemporaneous with, the pre-Pauline sending formula
in Gal. 4:4. It presents the sending of the Son as the eschatological
culmination of a series of previous missions, namely, those of the
Old Testament prophets. This indicates the origin of the "sending" concept. Originally it meant not the sending of a preexistent
being to earth, but the historical mission of key figures in Israel's

salvation history. It registers the divine initiative that marks that history. God raises up or sends people to fulfill his purposes, culminating in the sending of Jesus. Jesus himself certainly had a consciousness of mission, probably dating to the moment of his baptism by John.[21] Thus the sending-of-the-Son concept is rooted in the self-understanding of the historical Jesus. The development would be clearer if we had examples of the sending pattern with the image of servant or prophet. Unfortunately this is lacking in the primitive material. But we do have the kindred concept of God's "raising up" (with reference to historical mission, not to resurrection) Jesus as his servant or eschatological prophet in the kerygmatic passages (Acts 3:22 and 26).

W. Kramer has stressed that the sending-of-the-Son pattern always culminates in a purpose clause (*hina*) indicating the soteriological goal of the Son's mission (see Gal. 4:4; Rom. 8:3; John 3:17).[22] This is highly significant. The sending formula, while it calls attention to the beginning of Jesus' earthly career as the moment of God's initiative, nevertheless looks forward to its goal in Jesus' death and resurrection. In the final analysis, the sending schema has the same kerygmatic significance as the death/resurrection formula.

The sending pattern was one factor that shifted christological concern to the birth of Jesus. (The other factor was the Son of David christology).[23] The formula in Gal. 4:4 states that God sent his Son, "born of woman." While in itself this means no more than that Jesus was truly human, its effect was to focus attention on the moment of Jesus' birth. This focus becomes sharper in the formula in Rom. 8:3, "sending his own Son in the likeness of sinful flesh." Such a focus still remains within the orbit of the primitive eschatological prophet christology, for it is characteristic of the Old Testament prophets that they trace their call and sending to the moment of their birth or conception (Jer. 1:5, 7d; Isa. 49:1). Birth or conception is the moment when God predestines and elects a prophet in preparation for a concrete role in salvation history. It would probably be wrong to say that it is the actual moment of sending, for alongside the conception/birth motif we also have in the prophetic tradition the call story (*Berufungsgeschichte*). At the birth the call is planned and announced;

at the call it is set in motion. Here, perhaps, we see the factors that led to the retrojection of the Son of God christology to the moment of Jesus' birth, as has happened in the infancy narratives. The Matthean and Lukan annunciations express this retrojected christology in narrative form. They signify not the ontological status of Jesus but a call to the role that he is to perform in salvation history, a call which later will be actualized at the moment of the baptism. That is why Matthew and Luke can retain the baptism narrative with its voice from heaven despite the fact that they have already introduced Jesus at his conception/birth as the Son of God. The baptism narrative bears the same relation to the annunciation stories that the call stories of the prophets bear to their conception or birth. The same salvation-historical thinking underlies the prenatal annunciations of Ishmael, Isaac, and Samson. Thus we see that the retrojection of Son of God was not a mechanical process. It followed the pattern of Old Testament prophecy.

It has been widely held, especially among German scholars, that the Hellenistic conception of the divine man (*theios anēr*) played an important role in the development of the earthly Son of God christology.[24] Recent studies, however, suggest that the *theios anēr* is an artificial and largely synthetic product of the history-of-religions school.[25] Nevertheless, elements of the Hellenistic wonder-worker tradition have probably colored some of the gospel miracle stories and therefore contributed something to the meaning of the christological title Son of God as applied to his earthly life. An example of influence from this source would be the pre-Markan and pre-Johannine presentation of the miracles as epiphanies of the divine power of the Son of God. With the later development of incarnational christology, this epiphany concept became rather important, as we see in the Fourth Gospel. On the whole, however, it is the prophetic tradition that provides the strongest background of the miracle stories of the Gospels. Here the miracles are seen not as epiphanies of the divine but as signs of the inbreaking of the Kingdom. In performing miracles as Son of God, Jesus is prefiguring the redemptive work of his passion (Mark) or pointing to the revelation that will be accomplished in the glory of the cross (John). This is far more important to the evangelists than the *theios anēr* traits which have colored their traditions.

Summary

We began this chapter by probing the effect of Easter on christological reflection. We saw that the earliest community affirmed with assurance its tentative pre-Easter christological assessment of Jesus' earthly history. It did so in terms of a "theology of Jesus." Further, it postulated Jesus' ongoing exalted existence in heaven, thus continuing that "theology of Jesus" into a second stage. This is the "two stage" christology.

The two stages were characterized by two different sets of christological titles: Servant, Holy One, Righteous One, and Prophet for the earthly life; Christ, Lord, and Son of God for the heavenly stage. Since both sets of titles assert a theology of Jesus, this two-stage christology cannot be characterized as adoptionist in the later ontological sense of the word. The change of titles denotes a change of salvation-historical role.

In time, the postresurrection titles, Christ, Lord, and Son of God, were retrojected into the earthly life. Jesus died as Messiah. He was "anointed" as *Christos* and declared Son of God at his baptism (or transfiguration?). He was conceived and born already as Son of God. This retrojection does not entail the christologizing of a life previously regarded as unchristological or unmessianic. Rather, it involves the enlarging of the postresurrection titles to include the freight of the earlier earthly titles and images with roots in the self-understanding of Jesus.

FOR FURTHER READING

Brown, R. E. *The Birth of the Messiah*. New York: Doubleday & Co., 1977. Pages 29–32 and 311–16 should be read in connection with the retrojection of titles from the resurrection/exaltation to the baptism/transfiguration and finally to the birth/conception. Brown does not, however, connect the infancy narratives with the "sending" christology—largely, I think, because he is at pains on other grounds to dismiss any influence of the type of thinking behind Gal. 4:4 on the development of the birth traditions.

Hahn, F. *The Titles of Jesus in Christology*. London: Lutterworth Press,

1969. The most thorough treatment of its subject. Takes five titles in turn and traces the history of their use in pre-Christian Judaism, in the authentic Jesus tradition, and in the three strata of oral tradition before the written gospels. Hahn has been criticized for considering the titles apart from the context in which they are used and for his too rigid stratification of early Christianity into Palestinian, Hellenistic-Jewish, and Hellenistic-Gentile.

Kramer, W. *Christ, Lord, Son of God.* SBT 50. London: SCM Press, 1966. Supplements Hahn's *The Titles of Jesus in Christology* by studying three of the titles in the pre-Pauline material (and in Paul). Important for its analysis of the sending-of-the-Son formula.

Hengel, M. *The Son of God.* Philadelphia: Fortress Press, 1976. By means of one title, Hengel reconstructs the history of christological development from the first Easter to about 50 C.E. The years 30–35 C.E. saw the development of the two-stage or paschal christology and 35–50 C.E. of the sending and preexistence-incarnation christologies. It contains a vigorous refutation of the Gnostic redeemer myth and other theories of the history-of-religions school.

Tiede, D. L. *The Charismatic Figure as Miracle Worker.* SBLDS 1. Missoula, Mont.: Scholars Press, 1972.

Holladay, C. H. *Theios Anēr in Hellenistic Judaism: A Critique of the Use of this Category in New Testament Christology.* SBLDS 40. Missoula, Mont.: Scholars Press, 1977. Taken together, the above works of Tiede and Holladay constitute what in the view of many is a definitive refutation of the *theios anēr* (divine man) theory of the history-of-religions school as it has been employed as the key to some aspects of New Testament christology. Both works are doctoral dissertations and are quite technical.

NOTES

1. See above, pp. 18–23.

2. On Ps. 2:7 in pre-Christian Judaism, see J. A. Fitzmyer, *Essays on the Semitic Background of the New Testament* (Missoula, Mont.: Scholars Press, 1974; London: Geoffrey Chapman, 1971), pp. 116–17; cf. p. 153; also idem, *A Wandering Aramean* (Missoula, Mont.: Scholars Press, 1979), pp. 105–7: "It is now clear that Jewish apocalypticism was not unacquainted with the title 'Son of God,' but there is no evidence that it was associated with a *messianic* figure" (p. 113, n. 89).

3. W. Wrede, *The Messianic Secret*, Eng. trans. J. C. G. Grieg (Greenwood, S.C.: Attic Press; London: James Clarke, 1971), p. 216.

4. R. E. Brown, *The Birth of the Messiah* (New York: Doubleday & Co., 1977), pp. 29–32, 311–16.

5. R. H. Fuller, *The Foundations of New Testament Christology* (New

York: Charles Scribner's Sons; London: Lutterworth Press, 1965), has been criticized for suggesting this, and this reading of it appears to be supported by my assignment of three successive milieus (Palestinian, Hellenistic-Jewish, Hellenistic mission) to my three main types of christology (two foci, two-stage, and three-stage). I never thought of them as a straight-line, consistent development; the three types continue alongside each other, even in the same communities and in the same writers. But the three types must have emerged in that order.

6. See, e.g., Rom. 1:3–4, which apparently combines a two-stage christology with a three-stage christology.

7. For the connection between Jesus' baptism and his sense of mission, see J. Jeremias, *New Testament Theology* (New York: Charles Scribner's Sons, 1971), 1:49–56.

8. On the Jewish background of this title, see Fitzmyer, *Wandering Aramean*, pp. 115–42. Fitzmyer supports the view that the title is of Palestinian and Aramaic origin.

9. F. Hahn, *The Titles of Jesus in Christology* (London: Lutterworth Press, 1969), pp. 78–89.

10. Ibid., pp. 307–17.

11. Jeremias's oft-repeated claim that Jesus' use of *Abba* as an address to God was unique in Judaism has recently been criticized by G. Vermes and Morton Smith. For a judicious assessment, see J. D. G. Dunn, *Christology in the Making: A New Testament Inquiry into the Origins of the Doctrine of the Incarnation* (Philadelphia: Westminster Press, 1980), pp. 26–29. He concludes: *"The evidence points consistently and clearly to the conclusion that Jesus' regular use of 'abba' in addressing God distinguished Jesus in a significant degree from his contemporaries"* (p. 27).

12. Mark 13:32 and Matt. 11:27 par. Q might be held to offer multiple attestation. But each of these passages is itself open to suspicion as a later formation, the one apocalyptic in origin, the other wisdom-oriented. On Mark 13:32, see R. H. Fuller, "Demythologizing the Trinity," *ATR* 43 (1961), 121–31, esp. pp. 127–28. On Matt. 11:27, see J. M. Suggs, *Wisdom, Christology, and Law in Matthew's Gospel* (Cambridge, Mass.: Harvard University Press, 1970), pp. 84–95. Schillebeeckx is probably correct when he says "Jesus never spoke of himself as 'the Son of God' or 'the Son'; there is no passage in the synoptics pointing in that direction" (E. Schillebeeckx, *Jesus: An Experiment in Christology*, Eng. trans. H. Hoskins [New York: Seabury Press, 1979], p. 258). But at least it implies a unique filial consciousness not in terms of ontological identity but in terms of call and obedience.

13. On the transfiguration, see Brown, *Birth of the Messiah*, p. 315.

14. Cf. O. Cullmann, *The Christology of the New Testament* (Philadelphia: Westminster Press, 1959), pp. 64–82. Cullmann, however, traces this christology back to Jesus' *explicit* self-understanding (pp. 60–69), which involves an uncritical treatment of the evidence.

15. See above, note 7.

16. On this, see W. Kramer, *Christ, Lord, Son of God*, SBT 50 (London: SCM Press, 1966), pp. 115–25.

17. R. Bultmann, *Theology of the New Testament* (New York: Charles Scribner's Sons, 1951), 1:167, 304.

18. C. Colpe, *Die religionsgeschichtliche Schule: Darstellung und Kritik ihres Bildes vom gnostischen Erlösermythus*, FRLANT n.F. 60 (Göttingen: Vandenhoeck & Ruprecht, 1961). See also Dunn, *Christology in the Making*, pp. 98–99, and the literature therein, pp. 305–6, n. 3.

19. Thus E. Schweizer, *Beiträge zur Theologie des Neuen Testaments* (Zurich: Zwingli, 1970), pp. 83–95, esp. p. 92.

20. In R. H. Fuller, "The Conception/Birth as a Christological Moment," *JSNT* 1 (1978): 37–52, on p. 42, I overstated the case that Wisdom is never "sent" by God but always "comes" on her own initiative. As Dunn, *Christology in the Making*, p. 284, n. 153, has pointed out, Wisd. of Sol. 9:10 provides one exception. It is, however, still true that in the New Testament hymns the preexistent redeemer is never sent but comes on his own initiative.

21. See note 7.

22. See note 6.

23. On the Son of David, see Fuller, "Conception/Birth," pp. 38–39.

24. For a conveniently accessible summary of the "divine man" theory, see J. M. Robinson and H. Koester, *Trajectories Through Early Christianity* (Philadelphia: Fortress Press, 1971), pp. 216–19, and further literature in the footnotes; for a longer report, see C. H. Holladay, *Theios Anēr in Hellenistic Judaism*, SBLDS 40 (Missoula, Mont.: Scholars Press, 1977), pp. 1–15.

25. See Holladay's *Theios Anēr*, which is subtitled "A Critique of the Use of This Category in New Testament Christology."

5

Wisdom Traditions and Christology

Searching for the
Ontological Difference

We have seen that the initial expressions of Jesus' significance are soteriological. They point to his death and resurrection as the culmination of salvation history: the "first fruits" of the messianic age of salvation, or the reconciling of a sinful humanity. Jesus' preaching pointed to the presence of the rule of God which might be experienced in his ministry and which could also be considered a down payment on the future coming of that rule. At the same time, Jesus' ministry and his death push the question about Jesus' own identity and relationship with God into the spotlight. From its earliest formulations, the kerygma presents him as the messianic revelation of God, not simply as another in the line of teachers and prophets sent to Israel and rejected.

Within the narrative categories employed by most biblical writers, functional statements about people and about God's actions are the only ones available for describing their significance. However, other questions arise outside that narrative framework: "What makes Jesus different?" "How can he be worshiped as Lord?" Initially, such questions would be answered by telling stories about him or about the first disciples. Later, the influence of philosophical speculation about the nature of the divine and of the human mind or reason in relation to the divine, and about the possible origins of the universe, would lead to interpretations of Jesus and his role in creation and salvation that are not narrative at all but are stated in philosophical terms. The first-century Jewish philosopher Philo of Alexandria used allegory to provide such a philosophical translation for many of the Old Testament stories. Some of the philosophical traditions he used to create his great synthesis of the Bible and philosophy were apparently used by other Jewish thinkers in a less speculative fashion. They often provide our best parallels for terms and phrases that suggest the beginnings of such reflection in New Testament writings.

We must remember that this speculation is not a full-fledged acceptance of a philosophical system in any of the New Testament writers. As soon as we find terms from that speculation about wisdom, the divine Word, or the mind/soul, we should not jump to the conclusion that the author is presupposing a complete anthropology or cosmology to explain Jesus. These terms are used in an eclectic manner along with other images that still depend on the narrative mode of thought. They do not function as part of a philosophical system.[1] On the other hand, the New Testament writers' use of philosophical terms does indicate the desire to express the meaning of Jesus and salvation in ontological rather than in strictly narrative terms. We must, however, always be careful not to read later Christian theological reflection into the biblical beginnings. Perhaps the most difficult question to decide when approaching the interpretation of such passages in the New Testament is "Are the philosophical terms being used simply as variants for the functional language of biblical narrative, or do they represent the first attempts to formulate a language of ontology adequate to that revelation?"

Wisdom and the Life of Jesus

There are two different approaches to the question about the relationship of wisdom traditions and the life of Jesus. Some scholars have tried to reconstruct a wisdom myth from the convergence of Jewish wisdom traditions and Hellenistic myths about the Egyptian goddess Isis, who was acclaimed as the source of all cosmic order, as a universal savior. This myth would focus on Wisdom (Sophia) as a divine being who descends into the world to bring saving revelation to a lost humanity. In the second century, Gnostics put such materials together to formulate their stories of the fall/descent of Sophia into a world of darkness and the coming of salvation through the descent of a divine revealer. Christian Gnostics naturally identified the revealer with Jesus.[2] Some interpreters have tried to suggest that the Logos traditions of the Fourth Gospel are dependent on such a myth. The situation appears to be much more complex, however. The full-fledged examples of the myth do not emerge until the second century. At that point, we suspect that the narrative of such a story has itself been influenced by the Christian picture of Jesus.[3] Since there is no evidence for a full-fledged myth behind the various New Testament passages that use the language of wisdom theology, the parallels to the wisdom material are better understood as reflective categories. Rather than reconstruct a myth to tie them together, the exegete should ask how they are interpreted by the context in which they are used.[4]

The second source of wisdom materials occurs in the proverbs and sayings attributed to Jesus. Older reconstructions of the teachings of Jesus tended to focus on the eschatological sayings about the rule of God, since they represented the instances in which Jesus could be seen to differ both from his contemporaries and from the theological tendencies of Christians who preserved the sayings. Wisdom traditions and proverbs by their very nature do not fit the criterion of dissimilarity used in such analyses. Yet, the ubiquity of wisdom materials in the teaching of Jesus makes it difficult to suppose that all such sayings were later accretions.[5] Jesus' use of such wisdom sayings provides the basis for the picture of Jesus as a wisdom teacher which develops in the sayings-tradition. Prov. 8:1-6 describes Wisdom as a street preacher, calling out to humanity. The Q tradition has combined the image of Jesus as eschatological prophet with that of Jesus as Wisdom's spokesperson. The combination itself modifies the image of Jesus as spokesperson for Wisdom. As eschatological prophet, Jesus must be more than another wisdom teacher. He must embody the final revelation of Wisdom.[6]

The treatment of some of these Q sayings in Matthew marks a transition point in early Christian understanding of the relationship between Jesus and Wisdom. Jesus is clearly presented as Wisdom herself speaking (see Matt. 11:19 / / Luke 7:35; Matt. 11:25–30 / / Luke 10:21–22; Matt. 23:34 / / Luke 11:49; Matt. 23:37–39 / / Luke 13:34–35). Some scholars think that this identification of Jesus and Wisdom had become part of the sayings-tradition earlier than the writing of Matthew's Gospel and was part of the controversy about wisdom between Paul and the Corinthians. Whether that interpretation of 1 Corinthians is correct or not, the identification of Jesus and Wisdom is clearly reflected in the Matthean form of these Q sayings.[7] However, the christological significance of such an identification still remains open. The material involved gives no hint of Wisdom as an independent entity that has somehow "incarnated herself" in Jesus. Thus, this wisdom christology does not imply preexistence.[8]

The wisdom traditions provide a different interpretation of the passion from that common in the death/resurrection kerygma. Jesus' departure parallels the stories in which Wisdom withdraws from a humanity that refused to receive her (Prov. 1:28; 1 Enoch 42:1–2; 4 Ezra 5:10). The eschatological context provided by Q's picture of Jesus as eschatological prophet implies that this withdrawal is the final one. Wisdom will not send any more messengers (Matt. 23:38–39 / / Luke 13:35).[9] What of the identification of Jesus with Wisdom, then? Since these traditions lack any hint of preexistence, some scholars suppose that the sayings must be referred to the risen/exalted Lord as the embodiment of divine Wisdom.[10] However, the interpretation of the passion as the withdrawal of Wisdom suggests another route. The earthly Jesus as teacher of Wisdom is the final, full embodiment of God's Wisdom. That Wisdom has withdrawn from the world and is now preserved only among those "children" who have received it from Jesus.

Corinth and the Wisdom of the Cross

Paul's response to the problems created by wisdom speculation at Corinth seeks to modify the wisdom traditions by insisting on the priority of those symbols derived from the cross and resurrection of Jesus. The apostle's objections stem from the false implications about Christian life that follow from the Corinthian wisdom speculation. Its focus on wisdom as esoteric knowledge has encouraged the sectarian and divisive tendencies among the Corinthians. Some scholars think that Paul's addition to the formula in 1 Cor. 8:6—"through whom are all things and through whom we exist"—indicates that Paul preached a wisdom christology against the false views of the Corinthians. That christology makes Christ the mediator of creation as well as of salvation.[11]

This view runs into difficulties if one supposes that Paul advocates identifying Christ simply with Wisdom.

The Corinthians appear to have adopted a spirituality that sees Christianity as a way in which the soul achieves union with divine Wisdom. This union brings with it perfection, royal status, and immortality, the marks of the souls of really "wise men" of the Jewish tradition like Abraham and Moses.[12] The Corinthians do not seem to have drawn any christological implications from this unity of the soul with the divine. They appear to have thought that it was mediated at baptism by a particular apostle, a wisdom teacher such as Paul.[13] This view holds that Wisdom is the real agent of salvation, since it is in union with Wisdom that the soul receives its secure, immortal spiritual status.[14] Paul does want to replace Wisdom with Christ, since only Christ is the source of salvation.[15] To do so, he must make some important changes in the categories being used by the Corinthians. The paradox of the cross becomes the true Christian Wisdom; not the knowledge of Wisdom prized by the Corinthians.[16]

Since the cross is the true Christian Wisdom, Paul does not simply identify Christ and Wisdom in order to make his point about the source of salvation. The cross is the hidden Wisdom of God's action in reconciling humanity to himself. Other category changes must be introduced as soon as the eschatological perspective of the cross and resurrection becomes clear. Salvation is not achieved by individual, spiritual enlightenment, a process that may be perfected in a person here and now, as the Corinthians thought. The world is not simply a place from which the soul seeks its true nature and freedom by identification with the divine. Instead, the world, the people of God, and the individual Christian are still "in transit." The real transformation of our humanity and the conquest of death will occur only with the resurrection on the last day. Another feature of this eschatological perspective is Paul's repeated insistence that humanity and its wisdom remain under judgment. The most glaring evidence of the weakness of the Corinthian position appears in its inability to order the life of the community. The Corinthian interest in individual, spiritual attainment completely misses the obligations of love and concern for the other members of the community which are the foundation of the new people of God. Not only do the Corinthians make a mockery of their claims to wisdom and perfection, they risk judgment and condemnation as well.[17]

Wisdom and the Christological Hymns

The attribution of creative power to Christ in 1 Cor. 8:6 suggests that Paul and his audience are also familiar with ways of speaking about Christ which associate him with the creative side of Wisdom, as well as the soteriological side. These developments all appear in formulaic passages in the New Testament. That context implies that the language of such wisdom christology is first of all the language of confession and praise and not an attempt at precise philosophical articulation. As in the other examples of identification of Jesus with Wisdom, the exact import of the language applied to Jesus in these passages is hotly debated. While they are commonly cited as evidence for the claim that a preexistent, divine being is incarnated in Jesus, even that interpretation has recently been attacked as reading later christology back into the first decades of Christianity. Such a christology, critics argue, would require a more elaborate understanding of the triune God than could have been the case for imagery developed within the context of Jewish monotheism.[18]

Philippians 2:6–11

Philippians 2:6–11 contains a hymn to which Paul appears to have made additions, "death on a cross," "in heaven and on earth and under the earth," and the concluding doxology. Since it must have originated earlier than the writing of Philippians, it would appear to be our earliest example of a christological hymn. Unlike the other examples of such hymns, Phil. 2:6–11 does not associate the creative functions of Wisdom with Jesus. Instead it focuses on the contrast between divinity and humiliation in Jesus. It presents a striking contrast between the possibility of grasping equality with God and the super-exaltation of Jesus over the powers of the universe which followed his humiliation.

The three-part action of the hymn—equal to God, humbled himself, was super-exalted—suggests a narrative line which most interpretations of the hymn try to fill in by suggesting a story that lies behind the hymn. Some suggest that Jesus is presented as the New Adam, or that Jesus is the innocent righteous person of Wisdom 2–6, whose perfect obedience and death at the hands of evil people merits immortality. Some even suggest that the equality with God which Jesus does not take advantage of is the immortality owed to any person who is righteous and has not shared in the sin of Adam.[19] But the hymn itself resists being fitted into any prearranged story, as the controversy over this story makes clear. It faces us with the image of a human being who is exalted in a way that no other creature ever had been or could be again.

We can begin to appreciate the significance of the opening phrases about "grasping," "holding on to," or "taking advantage of" (depending on the translation one prefers for *harpagmos*) likeness to God, if we avoid becoming entangled in the debates about how such a thing could be said of the preexistent Christ and instead consider the human analogy that is implied. The desire to seize, hold on to, and take advantage of status and power was a fundamental fact of life in the competitive and hierarchical society of the time.[20] Public acknowledgment of the emperor as "like god," a great benefactor standing at the summit of that steep social pyramid, would reinforce the sentiment that "to be like god" was the summit of human worth.[21] A name was also an important indicator of status. Theft of a family name by an outsider was punishable by law. At the other end of this scale stood the slave, who was forced into a social position where another could command a person's very body, a position in which lying and flattery were a way of life if one was to survive.[22] Read with these common convictions in mind, the hymn speaks eloquently of the paradox of Jesus' life/exaltation. Paul's addition "death on a cross" intensifies the paradox implied by a life as "slave" on the part of a person the community knows to be divine. Further, the hymn concludes with a paradox, which Paul also heightens. The humiliated slave now rules the whole cosmos, with the divine name "Lord." Yet that rule is far from evident in the order of human affairs.[23]

Though the hymn does not directly identify Jesus with the activities of preexistent Wisdom, such an identification can only intensify the paradox presented by the hymn. Jesus' exaltation and cosmic rule would seem to call for such a confession. At the same time, the images of humiliation become all the more striking once "Wisdom" is introduced. This hymn makes another important christological point. Jesus' "slave form" is not to be attributed to his being human, bad luck, an accident, or even the hostility of his enemies. It is freely chosen by one who need not have done so, who had that "likeness to god" which humans might try to claim in moments of self-aggrandizement. Thus we begin to see the significance of the confession of Jesus' divinity emerge. It preserves the deliberate choice involved in his particular fate, and the possibility of seeing that choice as God's action in reconciling the world to himself.

Colossians 1:15–20

The opening section of the hymn in Col. 1:15–20 clearly associates Jesus with the Wisdom active in creation. Verses 15–18a would easily be understood by any audience as a reference to the creation of the world. The association of the cosmic "body," a Stoic metaphor for the cosmos, with the church might appear peculiar in its claim to identify a religious group with the cosmic body or the body politic. Several expressions used for Christ have ties to the wisdom tradition: "image of God" (cf. Wisd. of Sol. 7:26; Philo *Allegorical Interpretations* 1.43); "first-born of all creation" (Prov. 8:22, 25; and Wisdom as "first-born mother of all" [Philo *On Drunkenness* 30–31; *Questions and Answers on Genesis* 4.97]). Wisdom's presence before all creation is also a familiar theme. She is present at the creation (Prov. 8:27–30). God creates through her (Philo *Who Is the Heir of Divine Things?* 199).

Once again, one needs to know how to interpret the relationship between Jesus and Wisdom that is presented in the images of the hymn. Does it mean that he, not Wisdom, is to be identified with the creative Wisdom of God? Does it mean that Wisdom became incarnate in a human? Or is it without implications of preexistence but instead a metaphorical way of saying that Christ embodies the fullness of God's creative power or, in other words, that the divine Wisdom through which God created the world reached its completion only in the redemption won through Jesus? The hymn does not need to persuade a first-century audience that such divine power is operative in creation. Any number of philosophical and religious systems would agree to that. The turning point comes with the claim that that power is exhaustively embodied in Jesus and, further, that that creative power has reached a necessary completion in the salvation he brought. Thus the hymn makes an important christological affirmation: Salvation has cosmic significance because it belongs to, even completes, the creative activity of God. This perspective goes beyond the image of salvation as a "fix-it" job to rectify human mistakes. It challenges theologians to say how the creative and redemptive activities of God come together in Jesus.

Hebrews 1:3–4

Hebrews 1:3–4 appears to use hymnic phraseology. It comes from a writing with extensive parallels in Philonic traditions. The two verses allude to the creation-redemption-exaltation pattern that appears to be fundamental to the adoption of wisdom traditions in the christological hymn. Hebrews draws on a liturgical tradition that interprets Jesus' death as "purification for sins" and thus lacks the Pauline tradition's focus on the cross. Like the conclusion to Phil. 2:6–11, this section leads into the assertion that Jesus' exaltation is over that of all beings in the cosmos because of the name he has received. Three characteristics of creative Wisdom are applied to the Son: "reflection of the glory of God" (Wisd. of Sol. 7:26); "stamp of his nature" (Philo *On Planting* 18 ["stamp" = the eternal Logos]); and "sustaining all things by his powerful word" (Philo *Who Is the Heir of Divine Things?* 36; *On the Change of Names* 256).

Once again the focus of the passage is on the exaltation of Jesus, who has made purification and has been appointed heir of all things. The combination of the language of creation and salvation emerges when we recognize that in Philo "reflection of divine glory" and "stamp of divine nature" can also be applied to the human soul (*On the Creation* 146; *On the Special Laws* 4. 23; *Who Is the Heir of Divine Things?* 38, 181, 294; *The Worse Attacks the Better* 83; *Allegorical Interpretations* 3. 95–97). For Philo, the heir of divine things is the soul that has received the "stamp" of virtue and hence has realized its likeness to the divine. Here in Hebrews the heir is not just any virtuous human, but the Son, who has made purification for sin and been exalted above the angels. Much of the rest of the letter will argue that Jesus' unique sacrificial death is the only way for humans to achieve salvation, true sinlessness.

We see once again that wisdom language is concerned less with preexistence and creation than with salvation, with insisting that the only way to become "heir" is through Jesus, who embodies that divine wisdom.[24] This understanding of Jesus as "reflection of divine glory," as Wisdom, never interferes with the humanity of Jesus as known through the story of his life. Hebrews emphasizes the "sympathy" with which Jesus as high priest can deal with humanity (e.g., 4:14—5:10). Jesus is not characterized by the *apatheia* of the divine, or of the truly virtuous, in the philosophical tradition. Thus use of some of the traditional language about the divine character of the soul from Philo has not committed Hebrews to the whole pattern. His soteriology and his commitment to eschatology have led him to modify some of the conclusions that might have been drawn from his Philonic traditions.[25] The wisdom language that Hebrews uses does not dictate the whole of its christology. Instead, it serves as a vehicle to express the uniqueness of Jesus, when used in concert with other liturgical traditions and images derived from the Old Testament and from early Christian apocalyptic.

Summary

Wisdom traditions were used to enrich early Christian understanding of Jesus, his ministry, and his role in salvation on several levels. The sayings-tradition combined the wisdom sayings of Jesus with his eschatological call to recognize the impending rule of God. Jesus appears no longer as the conventional wisdom teacher instructing the youth but as the last messenger of wisdom to humanity. In that role, he appears as Wisdom herself, Sophia, making an appeal to humans. Identification of Jesus with Wisdom at this level does not yet involve a doctrine of preexistence. The soul of the wise or virtuous person can be described as identified with, marked by, or even married to Wisdom. The Corinthians seem to have taken up such a spirituality without any christological reflection. Paul counters their claims on many levels, not least by setting forth the crucified Christ as the paradoxical expression of true divine Wisdom. Hebrews may have been familiar with similar traditions about the soul of the wise/virtuous. It leaves no doubt that only Jesus, the Son and heir, represents the divine "stamp." Others can attain sinlessness only through his sacrifice.

The hymnic use of wisdom traditions broadens the language of salvation from eschatological focus on future righteousness before God to the present exaltation of the Lord and to the creation which reaches its fullness in him. The power of creation is the power of redemption. The suffering and death taken on by Jesus in redemption is not the "wages of sin" due him as human but a deliberate choice of divine power which is always greater than sin. Though still indirectly, we see that the Jesus who dies and is exalted cannot be fitted into any of the categories appropriate to other humans, even the most holy. Somehow this Jesus must be uniquely divine, more than a human. However incompletely New Testament authors express this insight, the development of the wisdom traditions makes it clear that it is the paradox of the divine acting/suffering as human, as Jesus, which merits exaltation and the "name above all names."

It should be clear from this discussion that the christological hymns do not present a full-fledged "preexistence" christology. They do not present Jesus as the incarnation of a discrete, divine person. Indeed, as Dunn has argued, it is inappropriate to use incarnation terminology to speak of the relationship between Jesus and divine Wisdom imaged in these hymns. They represent, however, a crucial stage in the development of christology, since these hymns begin to articulate the special relationship that exists between Jesus and God.

FOR FURTHER READING

Pearson, B. "Hellenistic Jewish Wisdom Speculation and Paul." In *Aspects of Wisdom in Judaism and Early Christianity*, edited by R. Wilken, pp. 43–66. Notre Dame, Ind.: University of Notre Dame Press, 1975). Pearson's chapter provides an excellent survey of the use of Jewish wisdom speculation in the Pauline writings.

Robinson, J. M. "Jesus as Sophos and Sophia: Wisdom Tradition and the Gospels." In *Aspects of Wisdom in Judaism and Early Christianity*, edited by R. Wilken, pp. 1–9. Notre Dame, Ind.: University of Notre Dame Press, 1975. Robinson's article surveys the various relationships between Jesus and Wisdom used in the gospel traditions.

Carlston, C. E. "Proverbs, Maxims, and the Historical Jesus." *JBL* 99 (1980): 87–105. Carlston surveys the use of wisdom sayings in the Jesus tradition. He argues that the historical Jesus must be seen as a wisdom teacher as well as an apocalyptic prophet.

Dunn, J. D. G. *Christology in the Making: A New Testament Inquiry into the Origins of the Doctrine of the Incarnation*. Philadelphia: Westminster Press, 1980. Pages 163–212. Dunn argues that one must approach carefully the question of the relationship between Jesus and Wisdom in the New Testament. Identification between Jesus and Wisdom did not necessarily imply preexistence. Often such identification asserts that God's creative and saving activity is embodied in Jesus.

Edwards, R. A. *A Theology of Q: Eschatology, Prophecy, and Wisdom*. Philadelphia: Fortress Press, 1976. Pages 58–79. Edwards describes the tradition of the sayings of Jesus which were preserved as the source of true wisdom.

Perkins, P. *Hearing the Parables of Jesus*. New York: Paulist Press, 1981. Pages 35–45. Perkins argues that many of the parables of Jesus have expanded materials from the Jewish wisdom tradition.

Suggs, M. J. *Wisdom, Christology, and Law in Matthew's Gospel*. Cambridge, Mass.: Harvard University Press, 1970. Suggs argues that Matthew has expanded the tradition of Jesus' wisdom sayings from Q into a full-fledged identification of Jesus and Wisdom.

Horsley, R.A. "Spiritual Marriage with Sophia." *VC* 33 (1979): 30–54. Horsley argues that Christians at Corinth sought salvation through direct experience of union with Wisdom. They did not identify Wisdom with Christ. Paul castigates them and introduces the paradox of the cross as source of salvation.

Bornkamm, G. "Understanding the Christ Hymn (Philippians 2:6–11)." In *Early Christian Experience*, pp. 112–22. New York: Harper & Row, 1969. Bornkamm presents the argument for a pre-Pauline hymn that acknowledged Christ as preexistent Wisdom behind this passage of Philippians.

Fiorenza, E. S. "Wisdom Mythology and the Christological Hymns of the New Testament." In *Aspects of Wisdom in Judaism and Early Christianity*, edited by R. Wilken, pp. 17–41. Notre Dame, Ind.: University of Notre Dame Press, 1975. Fiorenza questions the various attempts to find a comprehensive mythological pattern behind the christological hymns in the New Testament. She argues that their authors have made use of selected images and categories for reflective and not mythological purposes.

Murphy-O'Connor, J. "Christological Anthropology in Phil. II, 6–11." *RB* 83 (1976): 25–50. Murphy-O'Connor challenges the interpretations of Phil. 2:6–11 that see it as a claim to preexistence. He argues that the hymn is using wisdom traditions to present Jesus as the perfectly obedient righteous person who thereby gains immortality.

NOTES

1. Consequently, it is fair to say that Scripture does not dictate the philosophical categories theologians may use to explore the significance of Jesus, of salvation, or of God as presented in the Bible for our understanding of reality.

2. See G. W. MacRae, "The Jewish Background of the Gnostic Sophia Myth," *NovT* 12 (1970): 86–101.

3. See P. Perkins, "Gnostic Christologies and the New Testament," *CBQ* 43 (1981): 590–606.

4. See the appropriate distinctions made on this point by E. S. Fiorenza, "Wisdom Mythology and the Christological Hymns of the New Testament," in *Aspects of Wisdom in Judaism and Early Christianity*, ed. R. Wilken (Notre Dame, Ind.: Notre Dame University Press, 1975), pp. 17–41.

5. See C. E. Carlston, "Proverbs, Maxims, and the Historical Jesus," *JBL* 99 (1980): 91–99, who applies the criterion of dissimilarity to the topics about which Jesus speaks.

6. See J. M. Robinson, "Jesus as Sophos and Sophia: Wisdom Tradition and the Gospels," in *Aspects of Wisdom*, pp. 1–9; and J. D. G. Dunn, *Christology in the Making: A New Testament Inquiry into the Origins of the Doctrine of the Incarnation* (Philadelphia: Westminster Press, 1980), pp. 197–205.

7. See Robinson, "Jesus as Sophos and Sophia," pp. 9–14.

8. Ibid., p. 10.

9. Ibid., pp. 12–14. The withdrawal interpretation of the passion also appears in the *Gospel of Thomas* 38.

10. See Dunn, *Christology in the Making*, p. 205.

11. Ibid., pp. 165, 211.

12. See R. A. Horsley, "Consciousness and Freedom Among the Corinthians: 1 Corinthians 8–10," *CBQ* 40 (1978): 574–89; idem, "How Can Some of You Say That There Is No Resurrection of the Dead? Spiritual Elitism in Corinth," *NovT* 20 (1978): 203–31; idem, "Spiritual Marriage with Sophia," *VC* 33 (1979): 30–54.

13. See R. A Horsley, "Wisdom of Word and Words of Wisdom in Corinth," *CBQ* 39 (1977): 224–39.

14. Horsley, "Spiritual Marriage with Sophia," pp. 51–54.

15. Insofar as he does replace Sophia with Christ, Paul may be considered the founder of later mystical traditions in which the soul is betrothed to Christ; so ibid., pp. 30–32, 51–54.

16. See Horsley, "Wisdom of Word."

17. See Horsley, "Consciousness and Freedom."

18. See Dunn, *Christology in the Making*, pp. 170–76, and the provocative article that denies any preexistence allusions in Phil. 2:6–11 by J. Murphy-O'Connor, "Christological Anthropology in Phil. II, 6–11," *RB* 83 (1976): 25–50.

19. Even if one would not agree with the extensive parallels that Murphy-O'Connor, "Christological Anthropology," presupposes between this hymn and the story of the righteous and its implications of human immortality, one must acknowledge that we often read preexistence/incarnation into the hymn in a way that is not required by what it says.

20. See R. MacMullen, *Roman Social Relations* (New Haven, Conn.: Yale University Press, 1974), pp. 88–120.

21. See K. Hopkins, *Conquerors and Slaves* (New York and Cambridge: Cambridge University Press, 1978), pp. 210–19.

22. MacMullen, *Roman Social Relations*, pp. 108–9, 114–16.

23. Fiorenza, "Wisdom Mythology and the Christological Hymns," pp. 35–36, quite rightly stresses the importance of the hymn as a proclamation of cosmic lordship addressed to the Hellenistic world.

24. Dunn, *Christology in the Making*, pp. 206–9.

25. See G. W. MacRae, "Heavenly Temple and Eschatology in the Letter to the Hebrews," *Semeia* 12 (1978): 179–99, for another example of how Hebrews combines Philonic and apocalyptic traditions.

6

Mark as Narrative Christology

The Evangelist as Theologian

The development of redaction criticism over the past quarter century has led scholars to ask questions about the intentions and perspective of each evangelist. What is the situation of the community from which he writes? What is conveyed by the way in which he structures his material? What image of Jesus does he use to order the disparate images he has inherited from the traditions on which he draws to compose his Gospel? One method of answering such questions is to look for consistent patterns in the way an evangelist uses his traditional material. Markan scholars must use form-critical analysis to isolate sections in which Mark depends on earlier traditions, since they do not have written material with which to compare Mark, as in the case of Matthew or Luke.[1] A second approach relies on literary analysis, sometimes exclusively, sometimes in combination with the analysis of Mark's use of traditional material. The interpreter hopes to draw conclusions about the Markan perspective from the structure of the work as a whole. "Structure" can be defined in a number of ways: by a rhetorical analysis of the Markan text, by a claim that some other literary pattern forms the model for Mark, or by the uncovering of the "deep structure" of Markan narrative. It is not surprising that Markan scholarship is deeply divided over these approaches. We will look at competing accounts of Markan narrative and their bearing on the question of Mark's christology.

One of the most difficult questions faced by redaction criticism lies in its concern with theological categories. Some literary analyses criticize the exegetes for overinterpreting the literary features of narrative in their eagerness to exploit them as guides to an author's theology. For example, no one denies that the Markan

narrative contains elements of secrecy and even commands to silence about Jesus' identity. Since William Wrede, scholars have
labeled those elements as the "messianic secret" and used them as
the foundation for Mark's christology. Mark's image of the Messiah stresses hiddenness and suffering and is focused on the cross
even to the exclusion of the resurrection. However, a variety of
other traditions in Mark make it difficult to argue for "messianic
secret" as the sole christological perspective in the Gospel.[2] From
a literary point of view, one can argue that secrecy is a literary
feature of Markan narrative. The audience must share the secret
with the author while the protagonists in the story remain igno-
rant of it. Thus, secrecy in Mark should be understood as part of
the dynamics of the narrative presentation of author-audience,
not as the central feature in a theological construction.[3]

Tradition Analysis
and Christological Opponents

Many redaction-critical studies presume that the evangelist as-
sumes and shapes his traditions in opposition to the views of Jesus
held by others in the community and, perhaps, even implied in
the traditional materials the evangelist is using.[4] The most perva-
sive form of this hypothesis focuses on the miracle traditions in
Mark as indications of an opposing christology which presented
Jesus as miracle-worker, as filled with divine power. Those who
hold this view are said to be represented in the Gospel as the un-
comprehending disciples. Their christology makes it impossible
for them to see the truth of Jesus as suffering Son of Man. Their
failure is particularly glaring in the section framed by two stories
of the healing of blind men (Mark 8:22–26; 10:46–52). Though
they are instructed that the way of discipleship is one of suffering
and lowliness, not personal glory and exaltation, each passion
prediction shows them to be less and less able to understand what
Jesus is telling them (8:31–33; 9:30–32; 10:32–34). The stories of
the healing of the blind men form an ironic contrast to these disciples (= opponents).[5]

Other approaches to Mark try to solve the problem of its
diverse images of Jesus without canonizing one as "orthodox" and
the other (or others) as "heretical." They seek other ways of
bringing together the charismatic miracle-working on the one

hand and secrecy/suffering on the other. Howard Clark Kee proposes to accomplish this task by looking at Mark as an apocalyptic history.[6] The disciples represent the Christians of Mark's audience. Both are receiving secret teaching about the true significance behind the events narrated. The picture of Jesus in Mark is a highly stylized one. He appears as an itinerant teacher who interprets the will of God and whose powerful interpretation of God's will is also manifest in miracles. At the same time, the audience learns that the real triumph over evil comes in suffering. They should not be taken in by the attempts to seize and exercise power typical of the Palestinian scene in the late 60s C.E.[7]

Ecclesiology and christology cannot be separated in Mark. Jesus appears as the founder of this new community with its radical freedom from the Jewish Law and its openness to Gentiles. However, Mark does not distinguish Jesus' activities from those of his followers. They carry on, perhaps as wandering charismatic preachers, the activities he initiated. Thus, miracle-working, secrecy, and suffering are all characteristics of the Markan community, a small apocalyptic sect amid the turmoil of the years involving the Jewish revolt. This interpretation of the genre and purposes of Mark presents quite a different christology from that which focuses on the suffering Son of Man as the key to the messianic secret and supposes Mark to embody a Pauline understanding of the cross as the center of salvation. Instead, Jesus is presented as the model for discipleship. Charismatic powers enable his followers to triumph over evil. Their suffering and lowliness show that they do not seek or seize worldly power. They know that Jesus is to return as God's Messiah. Like other Jewish apocalypses, Mark is encouraging the elect to remain faithful.[8]

Scholars raise questions about this second approach because of its comprehensiveness. It does not distinguish traditional images of Jesus from the message that Mark directs to his audience. Paul Achtemeier argues that we must have evidence of deliberate Markan redaction of material if we are to speak about his purposes and draw conclusions about his own christology.[9] Suffering discipleship is clearly of central importance for the Gospel. This concern is evidenced both in the passion predictions and in the Markan formulation of the "whoever" sayings which follow

them (e.g., Mark 8:34–38). These sayings show Mark's preference for the title Son of Man over other christological titles. He
seems to prefer this title because of its association with the passion, not because of its apocalyptic overtones.[10] The apocalyptic
features emphasized in Kee's approach must be understood on the
basis of those sayings in which the Markan Jesus addresses commands of wakefulness to "all" and not just the disciples (as in
13:37). The expectation of the near parousia appears to have become problematic (cf. the repetition of 9:1 at 13:30). Perhaps, as
in 1 Thess. 4:13–18, deaths of members of the community have
caused this concern. Mark has formulated these sayings to reas-
sure Christians who are uncertain about the parousia.[11]

Finally, it is important to recognize that the powerful deeds of
Jesus do not represent the overriding image of Jesus in the Gospel.
Mark is equally concerned to present Jesus as a powerful teacher.
He edits the Sabbath saying in 2:27–28 to show that Jesus' words
have greater authority than the Law. Miracles as presented in
Mark are ambiguous. They do not lead those who witness them to
faith automatically. In fact, such people often become Jesus'
enemies. Mark edits 1:21–28 (in vv. 21–22, 28) to make it clear
that the power inherent in Jesus' teaching is the same power exhibited in his miracles. The Gospel provides several blocks of
teaching by Jesus (4:1–34; 7:1–23; 9:30–50; 10:17–31; 11:27–
12:44; 13:1–37). Mark 8:38 applies the Son of Man title to Jesus'
teaching, and teaching is the mode in which Jesus confronts his
enemies before the passion (11:27–12:44). Achtemeier agrees that
the traditions about Jesus circulating in Mark's community emphasized Jesus as miracle-worker.[12] His presentation of Jesus as
suffering Son of Man is part of a double correction of that image.
The other side of the correction is Mark's contention that the
power of Jesus is manifested in teaching as well as miracle-
working.[13]

The Structure and Meaning of the
Markan Narrative

Other approaches to Mark are less concerned with tradition and
redaction as the clue to Markan theology. They suggest that use of
literary methods to determine the underlying structure of Mark

will provide the key to the meaning of Mark as a whole. Though search for antecedents to the gospel genre has not shed light on the structure of Mark as a whole,[14] it may be possible to discover familiar literary patterns for different sections of the Markan narrative. George Nickelsburg suggests that many of the problems in interpreting Mark 11–15 are clarified if one recognizes the typical pattern of stories of persecution and vindication in Hellenistic Judaism behind these chapters.[15] The components of this pattern are:

1. *Introduction:* The protagonists are introduced and the situation of conflict is established. The first ten chapters of Mark serve as an introduction.

2. *Provocation:* A specific act by the hero provokes hostility. The cleansing of the temple in 11:15–18 is the first such action. Further provocation is attached to the anointing at Bethany (14:3–9).

3. *Conspiracy:* The response to provocation is the attempt to eliminate the hero. The first incident leads the chief priests and scribes to conspire against Jesus (11:18; 12:12–13; 14:1–2). The second incident brings Judas into the plot (14:10–11).

4. *Decision:* The hero must decide whether to remain faithful to God or submit to the pressure to abandon the purpose. Although the decision theme does not appear at this point in the Markan narrative, it has been introduced in the exchange between Jesus and Peter after the first passion prediction. The contrast between the two before the high priest emphasizes that decision: Jesus' messianic claim seals his fate; Peter's denial represents a decision to turn from discipleship. The taunt on the cross (15:29–32) is the final assertion of Jesus' decision to follow God rather than men.[16]

5. *Trust:* Sometimes the hero's decision is attributed to trust in God.

6. *Obedience:* Obedience to God seals the fate of the righteous person. Mark does not thematize trust and obedience separately, but they are implied in the accounts of Jesus' decision.

7. *Accusation:* The accusation against the hero may be true or, as in Mark, it may be a perversion of the truth.

8. *Trial:* Formal proceedings against the hero.

9. *Condemnation:* The proceedings lead to condemnation of the hero. Mark's Gospel contains two cycles of accusation, trial, and condemnation. The one before the high priest contains a true messianic claim in 14:62. The political trial before Pilate is only a perversion of the truth, which is answered by Jesus' statement "That's Pilate's opinion."

10. *Protest:* Though a formal protest of innocence is missing in Mark, the trial proceedings make that fact clear.

11. *Prayer:* The hero may protest innocence in the form of a prayer for divine vengeance or divine assistance. The judgment saying in 14:62 could be understood as a call for divine vindication, the words from the cross (15:34) as a prayer for assistance.

12. *Assistance:* Attempts to aid the innocent hero. Pilate's attempt to aid Jesus fits this element in the pattern (15:9–14). The flight of the disciples forms a sharp contrast to the expected attempt to aid the hero.

13. *Ordeal:* The truth of the hero's claims are tested in the ordeal to which the hero must submit. The Markan passion is presented as a messianic ordeal. Jesus' disciples may be imaged as part of that ordeal.

14. *Reactions:* The story is punctuated with reactions to the actions of the hero. The high priest rends his garments (14:63); Pilate is astonished at Jesus' silence (15:5).

15. *Rescue:* The hero may be rescued at the brink of death. Jesus is taunted to rescue himself, in a way similar to the challenge to the righteous person in Wisd. of Sol. 2:17–20.

16. *Vindication:* The essential elements in the genre are those that show the hero vindicated after all. It is introduced by the perception of the centurion that the crucified one is Son of God (15:39). The primary moment of vindication in Mark remains the parousia, when Jesus will be seen by all who have denied him (14:28; 14:62; 16:7).

17. *Exaltation:* Stories set in an earthly court have the hero

exalted to a high position. The righteous one who dies in
Wisd. of Sol. 2–5 is exalted to a high position in the heavenly court.

18. *Investiture:* Exaltation may include investiture with the
appropriate insignia (15:16–20).

19. *Acclamation:* Both investiture and acclamation have their
ironic counterparts in Mark. The "King of the Jews"
placard hints that Jesus has been enthroned on the cross
(15:26). Jesus has been invested with royal insignia by the
soldiers (15:16–20), and he is acclaimed by the centurion
(15:39).

20. *Reactions:* Those who see the exaltation of the righteous
person may voice further reactions.

21. *Punishment:* Those responsible for the hero's ordeal/death
are punished. Mark implies that that punishment will come
at the parousia. Thus the story awaits a temporal climax in
Jesus' return to Galilee, but the plot reaches its climax with
the exaltation/vindication of Jesus on the cross.[17]

The genre of the Markan passion narrative focuses our attention on the temple sayings as provocations. Typical of the genre,
Jesus' words are distorted into false accusation at the trial scene
(14:58) and by the crowd (15:29–30). Since the genre makes it
clear that such accusations are false, we may use that false accusation as a key to the situation which provoked the Markan narrative. The concerns of Mark 13 once again hold the clue. People
who claim to be "messiah" and who verify their claims with miracles appear to be gaining a following. They are preaching the impending eschatological destruction of the temple. Markan Christians should refuse to follow such people and flee from Judea. The
warnings about suffering and testimony probably refer to the consequences of that refusal. Thus the passion narrative does provide
a model for disciples to follow. They must also recognize that
Jesus' public vindication lies in the future.[18]

Others argue that the structure underlying a narrative must be
the expression of a pattern fundamental to narrative itself, a structure that is not determined by specific content, as in the previous
example. Such analyses are influenced by the development of

structuralist literary criticism in French intellectual circles. Dan
Via's attempt to apply structuralist insights to Mark leads him to
suggest that it belongs to a structure typical of the comic as such,
the triumph of life over death. He associates that comic genre
with the kerygma of death/resurrection as represented in Paul and
in Mark. Such a narrative opens up new possibilities for human
life. What appears to be the goal of a particular action is fulfilled
in its opposite.[19] See Figure 1. The symbolic patterns of the
Markan narrative mediate the experience of resurrection in the
only way that such a transhistorical event could be experienced:
through the symbols formed around it.

FIGURE 1

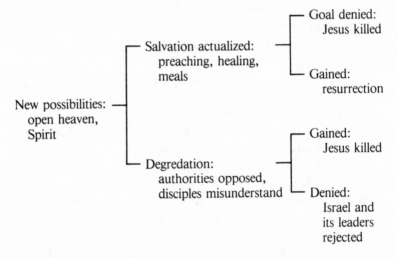

The standard syntagms of narrative sequence can also be found
semanticized in the story:[20]

1. *Need initiates action:* Lack of spirit in Israel; empty time;
   need of Kingdom.
2. *Disjunction:* Jesus (and disciples) leave family; baptism in
   crowd leads Jesus to wilderness (1:9–13). New community
   will be formed after the glorifying test.
3. *Qualifying test:* Wilderness victory over Satan provides Jesus
   with the helper needed to accomplish his task of mediating
   the Spirit and the Kingdom to Israel (new community; cf.
   1:14–15).

4. *Principal test:* The disciples' confession at Caesarea Philippi (8:27–30) indicates the beginning of the fulfillment of the need that initiated the action. It also shows Jesus' resolve not to relinquish suffering messiahship.

5. *Glorifying test:* Hero is recognized by his own. The transfiguration (9:2–8) proves insufficient until it is combined with the resurrection and parousia.

Individual sections of Mark can be broken down into narrative sequences that repeat the pattern of the whole. Much of the effectiveness of the narrative derives from the repetition of the underlying pattern on different levels. It would counter any sense that the life, suffering, and death of Jesus somehow belong to the tragic genre, are incomplete or a failure.

Mark as Narrative Christology

While the abstract categories of structural analysis deliberately avoid the specifics of content and hence the issues of interest to theologians, the call for attention to narrative does raise questions about the embodiment of christology in narrative. Nickelsburg's analysis of the passion narrative showed that earlier elements of the Markan account were necessary to fill out the relationships in the story. Similarly, many of the titles in that account already have their significance shaped by their use elsewhere in the Gospel. One question that has run through much analysis of Mark is that of audience identification. Narrative has the power to compel its audience to make judgments about themselves in light of what happens. Such identification is possible only if the audience sees themselves in the disciples.

Robert Tannehill has formulated one approach to appreciating the narrative dynamics of the Gospel by focusing on the interactions that take place within it.[21] The retrospective confession by the Gentile centurion is a key to the impact the whole story is meant to have on the reader; it is not simply an appreciation of the crucified. Jesus' own activity changes dramatically: His ministry is one of power and activity, but after the arrest it is strangely passive. Yet public use of christological titles of Jesus begins only when he has been rendered inactive with the confession at the first trial scene (14:61–62).

The interactions in the Gospel show a Jesus who does not affect all who encounter him in the same way.

1. The demons are destroyed. That destruction is not simply an eschatological sign. It also underlines the authority of Jesus' teaching (1:22, 27).

2. The scribes and the Pharisees initially function as the obstacles to Jesus. They oppose his forgiveness of sinners and his new eschatological freedom of action, which is evident in the proclamation of the primacy of the human over the Sabbath (2:1–3:6). In the final encounter, Jesus' powerful words frustrate them (11:27–12:44). Yet during his passion, these opponents ironically aid Jesus' goal of suffering messiahship while the disciples' misunderstanding appears to be the obstacle to Jesus. However, it is also important to recognize that in the narrative itself Jesus never becomes "enemy" to any of the groups that appear to hinder him.[22]

3. Supplicants come to Jesus to be healed. Healings occur only during the public ministry, and the injunctions to silence suggest that Jesus does not wish to be known by them.

4. The disciples are initially presented in a positive light. The audience should identify with them. But a pattern of anxious self-concern and fear develops (as evidenced in the three boat stories: 4:35–41; 6:45–52; 8:14–21). This pattern carries through the rest of the narrative. From 8:27 on, the passion kerygma shows that messiahship and discipleship can be formulated only in paradoxical terms. Jesus is the Messiah who suffers and serves; the King mocked by soldiers; the Savior who cannot save himself; the Prophet commanded to prophecy by his accusers even as the reader sees his prophecies unfolding in the passion.

This narrative perspective wants us to see that Markan christology is not limited to one theme or title. It depends on the unfolding impact of the story. None of the titles can express the paradoxes imaged in that story. More than one false estimate of Jesus is rejected along the way. Yet the final conviction of the story is that the disciples, who appear faithless, will become faithful. They will turn and follow the path marked out for them (14:28; 16:7).[23] The audience is to trust Jesus, because he has been shown to be trustworthy in the past.

Summary

Our sample of the divergent approaches to Markan theology shows that a great deal of work remains to be done before there will be anything like a consensus beyond the broadest outlines of suffering messiahship and discipleship as related themes in Mark. Some common threads appear in more than one approach, however. First, Jesus' teaching is to be given more prominence. It is a more important manifestation of his power and authority than the miracles he performs. Second, the question about Jesus' messiahship, "Who is Jesus?" cannot be separated from the question of discipleship, "What does it mean to follow Jesus?" Jesus has not been publicly vindicated against his adversaries. Consequently, the disciples are the only public witnesses to the exaltation presented in the passion story. Third, interpreters are increasingly convinced that the key to the situation of Mark's community is to be found in the troubles of Palestine at the end of the 60s C.E. Consequently, the christology of the Gospel must take into account the problems of false messianism, false prophecy, and suffering appropriate to that setting. What does belief in Jesus as Messiah or in his parousia mean for Christians living in those times?[24] The emphasis on Jesus' power and glory with which the Gospel begins is as important for Christian confidence in Jesus as Messiah as the portrayal of the paradoxes of a suffering Messiah and his disciples. Finally, the disciples cannot be cast simply as Jesus' (or Mark's) opponents. They are the medium for the reader to come into contact with the story, and they provide the terms in which the audience can apply that story to its own situation of discipleship.

Narrative by its very nature always suggests more than it spells out explicitly. Differences in presentation depend in part on those details to which a given interpreter or a given method is sensitive. Still, analysis need not be subject to every passing literary fad. Details of redaction and genre provide limits to the kind of assertions about Markan narrative which can be considered plausible. Narrative also provides something of an ongoing picture of relationships and activities that point to the identity of Jesus in a way that a mere collection of messianic titles or an abstract presentation of christology could never do. Mark challenges his readers to make the centurion's judgment their own.

FOR FURTHER READING

Kingsbury, J. D. *Jesus Christ in Matthew, Mark, and Luke*. Philadelphia: Fortress Press, 1981. An excellent brief introduction to the christological perspective of the synoptic gospels and Q. Kingsbury discusses each gospel's use of titles, its picture of the ministry of Jesus, its passion account, and its treatment of the themes of discipleship and community.

Achtemeier, P. J. "He Taught Them Many Things: Reflections on Marcan Christology." *CBQ* 42 (1980): 465–81. Achtemeier discusses the appropriate use of redaction criticism in determining Mark's christological views. He points out that Mark is not so preoccupied with the miracles source as some presentations suggest. Rather, he has been careful to present Jesus as teacher.

———. "The Origin and Function of the Pre-Marcan Miracle Catenae." *JBL* 91 (1972): 198–221.

———. "Toward the Isolation of Pre-Marcan Miracle Catenae." *JBL* 89 (1970): 265–91. These two important 1970 and 1972 articles by Achtemeier describe the methodology used to isolate pre-Markan sources and to evaluate their function.

Koester, H. "One Jesus, Four Primitive Gospels." In *Trajectories Through Early Christianity*, pp. 158–204. Philadelphia: Fortress Press, 1971. A typical defense of the view that Mark's christology of the suffering Jesus has been developed in opposition to the "divine man" christology of the miracle source.

Perrin, N. *A Modern Pilgrimage in New Testament Christology*. Philadelphia: Fortress Press, 1974. Pages 104–21. Perrin analyzes the use of Son of Man sayings in Mark. He argues that they reflect Mark's own christological concern for the paradox of Jesus as suffering messiah.

Weeden, T. *Mark—Traditions in Conflict*. Philadelphia: Fortress Press, 1971. Weeden interprets Mark from the point of view of the christological conflict that exists between the "divine man" of the miracle tradition and the suffering messiah of the Son of Man sayings and the Markan passion tradition. He presumes that Mark has shaped his gospel account against opponents who held the "divine man" view and are represented by the disciples.

Kee, H. C. *Community of the New Age: Studies in Mark's Gospel*. Philadelphia: Westminster Press, 1977. Kee argues that the message of a work, its literary form, and the type of community for which it is written all fit together. He suggests that Mark's theology is formulated from the perspective of an apocalyptic sect. Jesus has founded this sect, which holds the secret to the new age.

Nickelsburg, G. W. E. "The Genre and Function of the Markan Passion Narrative." *HTR* 73 (1980): 153–84. Nickelsburg shows the parallels between Mark's passion account and Jewish stories of the righteous person who is falsely condemned and then vindicated by God. Since this genre was well known, it serves to identify Jesus with such people.

Tannehill, R. "The Gospel of Mark as a Narrative Christology." *Semeia* 16 (1979): 57–95. Tannehill seeks to show that the interactions among groups in the Markan narrative carry important messages about Jesus' identity.

Via, D. O. *Kerygma and Comedy in the New Testament: A Structuralist Approach to Hermeneutic.* Philadelphia: Fortress Press, 1975. Pages 93–120. This structuralist approach finds the abiding universal pattern of the comic in the resurrection kerygma. Resurrection manifests the victory and renewal of life against all odds. Though Mark does not contain any resurrection visions, the whole Gospel can be seen to develop this fundamental pattern.

NOTES

1. See the careful analyses of the pre-Markan miracle catenae by P. Achtemeier, "Toward the Isolation of Pre-Marcan Miracle Catenae," *JBL* 89 (1970): 265–91; and idem, "The Origin and Function of the Pre-Marcan Miracle Catenae," *JBL* 91 (1972): 198–221; and his discussion of criteria for discerning which Mark is addressing his community in "He Taught Them Many Things: Reflections on Marcan Christology," *CBQ* 42 (1980): 465–69.

2. So R. Pesch, *Das Markusevangelium II Teil: Kommentar zu Kap 8, 27–16,20* (Freiburg: Herder, 1977), pp. 36–47. Pesch settles for a presentation of Jesus as eschatological prophet, bringer of the Kingdom, and final manifestation of the Son of Man. See the discussion of the Son of Man in Markan christology by N. Perrin, *A Modern Pilgrimage in New Testament Christology* (Philadelphia: Fortress Press, 1974), pp. 104–21. Perrin argues that the Son of Man passion predictions are Mark's own composition.

3. See the objections of F. Kermode, *The Genesis of Secrecy: On the Interpretation of Narrative* (Cambridge, Mass.: Harvard University Press, 1979), pp. 1–47.

4. As in H. Koester, "One Jesus and Four Primitive Gospels," in *Trajectories Through Early Christianity* (Philadelphia: Fortress Press, 1971), pp. 158–204.

5. See the sustained development of this hypothesis by T. Weeden, *Mark—Traditions in Conflict* (Philadelphia: Fortress Press, 1971).

6. See H. C. Kee, *Community of the New Age: Studies in Mark's Gospel* (Philadelphia: Westminster Press, 1977).

7. Ibid., pp. 103–5, locates Mark among the Greek-speaking villages of southern Syria during this period.

8. Ibid., pp. 136–44.

9. See Achtemeier, "He Taught Them Many Things," p. 467.

10. Ibid., pp. 471–72. Achtemeier questions the tendency to see Son of God as Mark's central title simply because it appears in the baptism, transfiguration, and crucifixion scenes. Its appearance there is likely to be traditional.

11. Ibid., p. 470.

12. Ibid., p. 481. The title Son of God may have been the primary christological title associated with those miracle traditions.

13. Ibid., pp. 472–76, which includes an extensive analysis of Mark's redactional use of terms for teacher. This image of Jesus' teaching differs from the picture in Kee, *Community of the New Age*, pp. 87–96, which makes Jesus a wandering charismatic teacher who calls disciples beyond the established social and economic boundaries of village life into the radical discipleship of an apocalyptic sect, a community of charismatic prophets (pp. 103–5).

14. See the survey of attempts in C. H. Talbert, *What Is a Gospel? The Genre of the Canonical Gospels* (Philadelphia: Fortress Press, 1977), pp. 1–40. Unfortunately Talbert has not been able to solve the problems of gospel genre either.

15. G. W. E. Nickelsburg, "The Genre and Function of the Markan Passion Narrative," *HTR* 73 (1980):153–84. Nickelsburg constructs his typology for the genre on the basis of Gen. 37ff., Ahikar, Esther, Dan. 3, Dan. 6, Susanna, Wisd. of Sol. 2–5, 2 Macc. 7, and 3 Macc.

16. Ibid., pp. 167–74. Nickelsburg suggests that 15:29–34 is an ironic portrayal of the conditions of discipleship, "whoever would save his life will lose it," in Mark 8:35.

17. Ibid., pp. 175–76.

18. Ibid., pp. 176–82.

19. See D. O. Via, *Kerygma and Comedy in the New Testament: A Structuralist Approach to Hermeneutic* (Philadelphia: Fortress Press, 1975), pp. 93–120.

20. Ibid., pp. 121–132.

21. See R. Tannehill, "The Gospel of Mark as a Narrative Christology," *Semeia* 16 (1979): 57–95.

22. The punishment of Jesus' false accusers is hinted at in the judgment oracle during the trial before the high priest (14:62).

23. Tannehill, "Mark as a Narrative Christology," pp. 84–85, argues against those who see these sayings as references to the parousia. He understands 16:8 to imply that failure is still possible for the postresurrection community.

24. Thus, however one reconstructs the opponents of Mark, they should not be assimilated into the *theios anēr* type of opponents postulated for 2 Corinthians as Koester ("One Jesus," pp. 189–91) tries to do.

7

Christology in Matthew
and Luke

The title of this chapter is chosen advisedly: "christology *in*
[not *of*] Matthew and Luke. In our opinion, neither Matthew nor
Luke is concerned about christology as such. In this way they
differ from Mark and John, both of whom were confronted with
situations that called forth a direct christological response.

Matthew

Not everyone agrees that this is true of Matthew. The leading
Protestant Matthean scholar in the U.S.A., Jack D. Kingsbury,
does hold that Matthew's primary concern *was* christological.[1] He
bases this view on an analysis of the structure of Matthew's narrative. He finds the clue to this in the two occurrences of the phrase
"from then" (*apo tote*) which punctuate the narrative at 4:17 and
16:21. This enables him to divide Matthew into three parts, 1:1–
4:16, 4:17–16:20, and 16:21–28:20.[2] The first part presents
Jesus as Messiah, the second part the public ministry of Jesus,
and the third part Jesus' passion, death, and resurrection. Son of
God is for Kingsbury the central christological title that covers all
three parts of the Gospel. Jesus was born as Son of God; he carries
out his public ministry as Son of God; and he suffers, dies, and is
raised again as Son of God. Other titles are used—notably Son of
David, Son of Man, and *Kyrios*—but all these are subordinate to
Son of God. Matthew's purpose, states Kingsbury, is to set forth
the salvation-historical meaning of Jesus for both Jews and
Gentiles.

Impressed as we are by Kingsbury's learning and exegetical insights, we remain unpersuaded by the force of his arguments. Our

reasons are as follows. First, too much weight is placed on the occurrences of *apo tote* ("from then") in determining the structure of Matthew. It is true that it occurs at important junctures of the narrative—4:17, at the beginning of the Galilean ministry; 16:21, at the first passion prediction. But it also occurs at 26:16, at the conclusion of the paragraph on Judas's compact with the sanhedrin, which is not nearly so decisive a turning point in the Gospel as a whole. Second, Kingsbury's suggested *Sitz im Leben* for Matthew is imprecise and too general.[3] Indeed, it could be applied equally to most of the New Testament documents. Third, Kingsbury too easily dismisses a more obvious clue to Matthew's structure, namely, the fivefold formula "It came to pass when Jesus finished [a discourse]" to which B. W. Bacon called attention many years ago. Few people today would buy into Bacon's thesis that Matthew deliberately structured his Gospel as a new Pentateuch with five discourses, and many objections have been raised against it. Not all these objections, however, are of equal weight. Some scholars have asked, for instance, how the passion narrative fits into this scheme. The answer is that both the infancy narrative at the beginning and the passion-resurrection narrative at the end stand outside the fivefold scheme. The five major sections occur between the prelude and the climax, each section consisting of a discourse preceded by narrative material.[4]

A clearer view of Matthew's *Sitz im Leben* is suggested by W. D. Davies,[5] who links it with the developments in Palestinian Judaism after the fall of Jerusalem. Between 80 and 90 C.E. (i.e., during the decade in which Matthew was written), members of the Pharisaic party gathered at Jamnia and carried out a series of reforms that made Pharisaic Judaism normative. In the process they eliminated all competing varieties of Judaism, including the Jewish-Christian. They excluded Jewish Christians by inserting into the liturgy the *Birkath ha-minim*, which included a curse on the *Nosrim* (Nazarenes).[6] Matthew's Gospel contains material that reflects various tensions between Jewish Christians and Jews; there were both persecutions and martyrdom (see Matt. 10:17–39, a redactional conflation of material from the Markan apocalypse and Q). Mission to the Jews was becoming increasingly difficult. It may not have been abandoned, as Douglas Hare thinks,[7] but certainly the Jewish Christians have at last decided to turn to the Gentiles (Matt. 28:16–20), thus following the Pauline churches some forty years later.

In this situation, Matthew seeks to buttress the morale of his Jewish Christians by assuring them that in Jesus they, not the rabbis of Jamnia, have the true exposition of the Mosaic Torah, that they are the *true* Israel and as such will be judged at the End by the standards of the Torah as expounded by Jesus.[8] In other words, Matthew's main interests are in the Law, in ecclesiology, and in eschatology,[9] rather than in christology.

The true interpretation of the Torah is expounded in the five books in which Matthew structures the central part of his Gospel, and it comes to expression especially in the Sermon on the Mount. The Law is comprehended in the double love commandment (22:37–39) or the Golden Rule.

Matthew's ecclesiology is set out principally in Book 4 (Matt. 13:53–19:1), which contains among other things the allegory of the boat (Matt. 14:13–27), the "Thou art Peter" pericope (Matt. 16:17–19), and the community discourse (chap. 18). The eschatology in turn is set forth in Book 5. The eschatological discourse includes the whole of Matthew 23–25. Some scholars have objected to taking the discourse as a single whole on the ground that there is a change of scene between chapters 23 and 24. But Matthew is capable of changing scenes in the middle of a discourse, as he does in chapter 13 (see vv. 13, 34, 36). And the denunciation of false teachers at the conclusion of the document is characteristic, as Günther Bornkamm has pointed out in connection with 2 Corinthians 10–13.[10]

Matthew's christology is therefore not a subject in itself but something that arises out of his primary concerns for the Law, ecclesiology, and eschatology. We see this happening negatively in Matthew's redaction of Mark. He is not nearly as concerned as Mark is with polemic against those who ignore or soft-pedal the cross. Note, for instance, Matthew's rewriting of the confession of Peter so that "Thou art the Christ" becomes a positive, acceptable confession, not an inadequate one that must immediately be qualified by the passion prediction. Indeed, Matthew detaches the prediction from the confession pericope by an *apo tote*. Similarly, Matthew tones down the messianic motif, for instance, in 12:15–21, where he sees the command to silence in the miracle stories as the fulfillment of Isaiah 53.

Again he tones down the disciples' misunderstanding. A striking example of this is the disciples' reaction to the parables. In Mark they are reduced to incomprehension, but in Matthew, when Jesus asks them if they have understood the parables, they blithely answer, Yes! (Matt. 13:51). The disciples at worst are just *ologopistoi*, men of *little* faith, not complete nitwits (e.g., Matt. 8:26).

Mark had taken great pains to construct his central section (8:27—10:45) on a threefold pattern of passion prediction, disciples' misunderstanding, and teaching of the cost of discipleship. One *apo tote* (16:21) comes right in the middle of this Markan section, which shows how Matthew has dismantled it. The community discourse (Matt. 18) and the parable of the laborers in the vineyard (20:1–16) also disturb the Markan pattern. Finally, the introduction of much teaching material from Q and special Matthew results in a serious diminution of the proportion between ministry and passion narrative.

On the positive side, Matthew presents Jesus first and foremost as a Moseslike figure, a procedure wholly intelligible in the light of Matthew's *Sitz im Leben*. The infancy narrative recapitulates the stories surrounding Moses' birth.[11] Like Pharaoh with the Hebrew children, Herod sought to slay the innocents of Bethlehem (2:16). Like Moses and Israel, Jesus came up out of Egypt into the Holy Land (2:19–23). Thus Matthew relocates the Great Sermon on "*the* mountain" so as to parallel the lawgiving on Sinai (5:1). The transfiguration on the mountain is full of Mosaic themes, and Moses precedes Elijah (17:3), rather than tagging along with him as in Mark. The great charge likewise takes place on "the" (not "a") mountain (28:16). It is even possible, as some have thought, that Matthew has deliberately placed ten miracles in chapters 8 and 9 to correspond to the ten plagues of Egypt.[12]

Within the context of the Law, ecclesiology, and eschatology, much of Matthew's christology is apologetic and directed toward the Jamnia party. The term *Christos* is used fourteen times, together with the following equivalents, all of which are conceived in terms of Old Testament fulfillment: Son of David (seven times), together with a genealogy highlighting Jesus' Davidic descent; Emmanuel (1:23); King (of the Jews) six times; the Coming One (11:3). This royal motif, however, is reinterpreted and is not a political messiahship. The miracles fulfill the portrait of the suffering servant in Isaiah 53 (8:17). Jesus' entry into Jerusalem is interpreted by the fulfillment citation of Zech. 9:9. The parables fulfill Isaiah 6 and Ps. 78:1 (Matt. 13:14–15, 35). Then, on a broader canvas, there are the fulfillment citations that punctuate both the infancy narrative and the passion narrative. In Jesus, Israel's history reaches its climax and fulfillment. In him the promises to Abraham as well as to David reach their goal.

The title Son of God occurs twelve times in Matthew. Of these, six are from Mark, two are from Q, two (14:33 and 16:16) are probably due to conflation of non-Markan tradition with Markan material, and one occurs in a fulfillment citation (2:15). The only occurrence that is clearly redactional is 27:41, the observation of the crowd at the cross about Jesus' claims, so impressively treated in Bach's *St. Matthew Passion*. The paucity of occurrences in indubitably Matthean redaction militates against the importance assigned this title by Kingsbury. It is hardly the key title, though it is certainly an important one. For Matthew it is the characteristic Christian confession which the Jamnia Jews rejected.

Matthew has also included five wisdom sayings from Q (11:19; 11:25–27; 11:30; 23:34–35; 23:37–39). Jack Suggs and Felix Christ have argued that Matthew advances beyond the Q christology of "Jesus the eschatological spokesman of wisdom" to "Jesus as the incarnation of wisdom."[13] Caution, however, is advisable. The term "incarnation," strictly speaking, implies preexistence of a divine being who takes on human form. As we saw in Chapter 6, Matthew's christology has not reached that point of development. He is innocent of any preexistence motif. The most we can say is that God's wisdom (that is, a personified aspect of his activity), which had been at work all through Israel's history, is now definitively operative in Jesus. We might say that Jesus "incarnated," or embodied, God's wisdom (or perhaps, with Eduard

Schweizer, the Torah), but hardly that he was the incarnation of wisdom. Between him and wisdom there is a coincidence of operation, not an identity of person.

The most frequently used title in Matthew is Son of Man, which occurs some thirty-two times. Of all the titles that may claim to be central in Matthew, this surely is the one. Twenty-one of the occurrences are from Markan or Q material. Nine are either special Matthew or Matthean redaction. Six of these are apocalyptic and go back to the tradition that begins with Dan. 7:13. Danielic imagery is further used in Matt. 28:16–20 with the reference to "all authority" being granted to the Resurrected One. How does Matthew's predilection for Son of Man as a christological title relate to his overall purpose and *Sitz im Leben*? I suggest that this expresses opposition to the role of Moses in post-Jamnia Judaism. The Son of Man's career, especially his death and resurrection, founds the true Israel. He rules the true Israel (= the kingdom of the Son of Man, 13:41) in accordance with his true exposition of the Mosaic Torah now. And he will judge the true Israel at his coming again in accordance with the prescriptions of his exposition of the Torah. It is therefore arguable that the Son of Man is the key title in the Gospel of Matthew.

Luke

It has long been held that Luke is primarily a historian. Today we should qualify that. His historical interests should not be confused with mere historicity. He is a theologian of salvation history. His historical perspective leads him to situate the Christ event in a particular time and space, precisely as an event of salvation history. His christology is set in that framework. It is aimed at showing that the Christ event implies a universal salvation. As we shall see, he makes use of a large number of titles, many of them quite primitive, in the telling of the story of salvation. Luke has "retold the Jesus-story with a definite christological and soteriological slant: what Jesus did, said and suffered had and has a significant bearing on human history."[14]

But what is the precise pattern of salvation history which provides the framework in which Luke sets his christology? Hans Conzelmann, one of the pioneers of the redaction-critical treatment of Luke, thought that Luke divided salvation history into three periods: the period of promise, covered by the Old Testament; the "center of time," that is, the Jesus period covered by the Gospel; and the period of the church, covered by Acts.[15] Luke regarded the Jesus period as one of eschatological fulfillment (Luke 16:16), but the period of the church, like the Old Testament period, is again historical and noneschatological. Eschatological reality ascends, as it were, with Christ at his ascension. Conzelmann's characterizing of the third period is open to criticism.[16] The major objection is that Luke characterizes the period of the church as the period of the Spirit, and the Spirit is itself an eschatological reality. In fact, Luke goes out of his way to underline this in his citation of the Joel passage in Acts 2:16–21, where he inserts the words "in the last days" before "I will pour out my Spirit" (v. 17; contrast Joel 2:28). Moreover, the opening verse of Acts (1:1) implies that the second volume is the story of what Jesus *continued* to do and to teach after his ascension, just as the first volume consisted of what he *began* to do and to teach. We would therefore retain Conzelmann's three periods, but characterize them differently:

> Period 1: promise[17]
> Period 2a: what Jesus began
> Period 2b: what Jesus continued

Conzelmann also divided the Jesus period into three:

> Luke 3:1—4:13—the initial struggle with Satan
>
> eschatological $\begin{cases} \text{Luke 3:23—22:2—the "Satanless time"} \\ \text{Luke 22:2–24—the final struggle with Satan} \end{cases}$

The designation of the middle period of Jesus' ministry by the curious term "Satanless" is based on a dubious interpretation of "an opportune time" in 4:13.[18] A glance at a concordance will show that Satan is mentioned at 10:18 as having fallen from heaven as a result of exorcisms—in this context the exorcisms of Jesus' disciples on their mission (see also 11:18 and 13:16). Luke no less than the other synoptists sees the ministry as a continuous conflict with Satan.

If we are to divide the Gospel into three periods, it would be better to allow the structure to be determined by geography. In fact, Luke is a geographer as well as a historian of salvation history. Accordingly, we divide the ministry of Jesus as follows:

1. Galilee: 4:1—9:50
2a. The journey to Jerusalem: 9:51—19:27
2b. Jerusalem: the passion, death, and resurrection: 19:28—24:53

These two schemas will provide a framework for Lukan christology.

Luke's christology fits in neatly with the two-stage christology of the early community. It is interesting to find Luke staying with a more primitive christology at a time when the other communities (e.g., the Pauline and perhaps also the Johannine) with which he (or the traditions he utilizes) was in contact had developed much further. The christological pattern of the Gospel of Luke is shown in Figure 2.

FIGURE 2

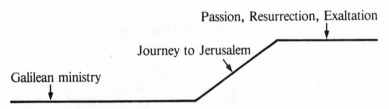

A succinct summary of Luke's two-stage christology erected on this framework is found in the logion "Was it not necessary that the Christ should suffer these things and enter into his glory?" (Luke 24:26). *Per ardua ad astra!* The travel section of the Gospel is a kind of coronation procession. Jesus is proceeding to Jerusalem, the place where his "assumption" (*analēmpsis*) is to occur (9:51). This is the "exodus" that he was to accomplish in Jerusalem (9:31).

Some of the christological titles Luke uses apply exclusively to the first stage, the ministry and the passion.[19] Among such titles is Prophet. In 4:24 and 13:33 this title appears on the lips of Jesus as an indirect self-designation. In 7:16 it appears in the testimony of the crowd, "A great [the eschatological] prophet has arisen among us," and "God has visited his people." Notice that here we still have a theology of Jesus rather than a christology per se. In his inaugural address in the synagogue at Nazareth, Jesus is the eschatological prophet who was anointed with the Holy Spirit to fulfill the prophetic role of proclaiming and enacting the eschatological liberation of the poor and oppressed. He had already been marked out from his conception for this prophetic role, as Luke indicates by modeling Jesus' birth on the birth stories of the prophets, such as Samuel. Some scholars have thought that Luke models Jesus on the pattern of the pagan divine man (*theios anēr*).[20] Luke has certainly admitted some traits of the divine-man concept, which was natural enough considering the Gentile environment in which he wrote. This comes out particularly in his handling of Jesus at prayer. In Mark, Jesus prays at moments of crisis concerned with the problem of the messianic secret (Mark 1:35; 6:46). In Luke he prays to replenish his *dynamis*, his miraculous powers, which have been drained from him in the performance of his healings (Luke 5:16; 9:18). These *theios anēr* traits are, however, subordinated to the prophet motif.[21] Jesus also prays at temporal and geographical turning points in his history (Luke 3:21; 6:12; 9:28), which shows that the salvation-historical perspective is paramount to Luke's thinking.

A striking mode of address is Luke's use of Master (*epistatēs*). The disciples always address Jesus as such, never as teacher (contrast Mark). For Luke, Jesus is neither a rabbi nor the founder of a philosophical school. "Master" suggests not Jesus as instructor but his charismatic authority, and it is closely akin to Prophet.

Luke's use of Servant (*pais*) is, surprisingly, confined to Acts. It denotes not the *suffering* servant but God's chosen agent in salvation history, like Abraham, Moses, David, and Israel.

It is characteristic of Luke that he uses many of the christological titles to straddle the two stages of his christology of Jesus, thus reinforcing his theme "through suffering to glory" as the pattern of salvation history. In using Son of Man in this way he is following his Markan model (*Vorlage*). At the same time, he uses it in a significant logion emphasizing the lowly *service* of the earthly Jesus, the basic pattern in which Luke formulated his soteriology (Luke 19:10; cf. 22:24–27). At the same time, he uses it at the

moment of Stephen's martyrdom to signify Jesus' present exaltation (Acts 7:52). It is precisely at the moment of his own martyrdom that Stephen sees Jesus as the Son of Man at the right hand of
God: through suffering to glory.

The title Son of God likewise straddles the earthly and heavenly
stages of Luke's christology, but it is used in different ways for
the two stages. Luke can do this because for him Son of God still
denotes a role in salvation history. At his birth Jesus is destined
for that role (Luke 1:32, 35). At his baptism he is invested as Son
of God (Luke 3:22). At his ascension he is enthroned as such.
Until then no human being acknowledges Jesus by that title. Note
particularly Luke's replacement of Mark's "Son of God" on the
lips of the centurion at the foot of the cross with "innocent man"
(Luke 23:47). The baptismal investiture takes effect in two
stages. In the earthly ministry Jesus is the anointed prophet servant ("with thee I am well pleased," echoing Isa. 42:1), while the
royal aspect of the Son of God title does not take effect until the
exaltation (Acts 13:33). Once again we see in this title the
salvation-historical framework of Luke's christology.

The situation is similar with the title Son of David. Jesus is
born of Davidic descent (the infancy narrative and the genealogy),
but this only *qualifies* him to reign as Davidic Messiah. His actual
reign as such is inaugurated at the exaltation (see Acts 2:24–31,
which applies the Davidic Psalm 16 to the risen Jesus).

It is remarkable that a late (apparently Gentile) author such as
Luke can still use *Christos* as a title, rather than a proper name.
This title, too, straddles the two stages of Jesus' career. He is the
Christ from birth (2:11), yet he is appointed the Christ at his enthronement (Acts 2:36). He suffers as the Christ and then enters
into his glory (Luke 24:26, 45). How do we reconcile these con-
fusing statements? It is tempting to suppose that Luke has incor-
porated earlier traditions from various stages of development and
used them promiscuously, but that would be unfair. Once again,
salvation history provides the clue. At his birth Jesus is *destined*
for his messianic role. At his baptism he is *invested* as the eschatological prophet, and so in one sense is already functioning as
Christos. At his death he passes as royal Messiah designate to the
glory into which he is finally installed at his enthronement.

Like *Christos*, the title *Kyrios* is used both for the earthly Jesus and after his ascension. In the earthly period it is especially prominent in narrative. Luke apparently finds it used frequently in his special source and inserts it redactionally in his Markan material. Yet, as with *Christos* so with *Kyrios*: God appointed him Lord at his ascension (Acts 2:36). Luke also uses it for the returning Christ in his allegorized eschatological parables (e.g., 12:37). How are we to reconcile these various usages? Once again Luke is thinking in functional, salvation-historical terms. In his earthly life, Jesus was Lord in the sense of the anointed eschatological prophet. At his enthronement he becomes the ruler of the church, of its life and mission, and at the end he will come as cosmic judge (and savior).

There are two titles that seem to speak of the transition from the earthly stage to the heavenly stage. The titles in question are Savior and Author (*archēgos;* better "pioneer"). Savior, it is true, appears twice in the infancy narratives and therefore could be taken as an earthly title as well, but it is never used in the ministry. Accordingly, it probably refers in the infancy narrative to the ultimate destiny of the child at his exaltation and parousia. *Archēgos* is used particularly of Jesus' passing through suffering to glory.

Perhaps it is significant that Luke uses no titles exclusively for the exalted stage of Jesus' work. This is the case, we suggest, because for Luke the heavenly stage depends entirely on the earthly stage. Jesus became what he is by doing what he did. Only the humiliated and suffering Christ could enter into his glory. The titles bring out the interlocking of the two stages of salvation history. The earthly stage is not left behind by the heavenly—which argues powerfully against Conzelmann's interpretation of Luke's salvation history and those interpretations that would deny to Luke a theology of the cross.

Summary

Neither Matthew nor Luke is concerned primarily with christology. Matthew, responding to the situation created by Jamnia, seeks to present the church, over against the synagogue, as the true Israel of God, living under the Torah as expounded by Jesus. He founded the church and will judge it according to the standards of his own interpretation of the Torah when he comes again.

Of the various titles Matthew uses, Son of Man seems to be most prominent, and it embraces all three of Matthew's primary concerns: Jesus founds the church as Son of Man through his death and resurrection; as Son of Man he promulgates the eschatological interpretation of the Torah; as Son of Man he will come again as judge of the church.

Luke is preeminently the theologian of salvation history. He divides salvation history into three periods. The first is the time of promise (the Old Testament, summed up in the infancy narrative). The second and third are both Jesus periods: first the ministry, then the exalted life of Jesus after his resurrection and ascension. Also, Luke divides the earthly activity of Jesus into three periods: the Galilean ministry, the journey to Jerusalem, and the "exodus" or transition from earth to heaven. In so doing, Luke brings out the pattern: through humiliation and suffering to glory.

Luke's use of the christological titles corresponds to these threefold divisions of salvation history. One set is used exclusively for the earthly ministry: Prophet, Master, and Servant. Another set straddles the earthly and the heavenly phases of Jesus' activity: Son of Man, Son of David, Christ, and Lord (*Kyrios*). Despite appearances to the contrary, Luke does not use these titles promiscuously. They have different senses, corresponding to the two Jesus periods. Finally, two titles are used to cover the transition: Savior and Author (Pioneer). No titles are used exclusively of the heavenly stage. This is significant, for Luke never relegates the earthly ministry and the passion to the past; it is always through suffering to glory. Therein lies the *theologia crucis* which his christology articulates.

FOR FURTHER READING

Matthew

Kingsbury, J. D. *Matthew: Structure, Christology, Kingdom*. Philadelphia: Fortress Press, 1975. The most important study of Matthew's christology now available. On the basis of a threefold division of Matthew (*contra* B. W. Bacon's fivefold division) punctuated by the use of *apo tote* (from that time) at 4:17 and 16:21. Kingsbury holds that Son of God is Matthew's most important title.

Ellis, P. F. *Matthew: His Mind and His Message*. Collegeville, Minn.: Liturgical Press, 1974. Includes a brief study of Matthew's use of the christological titles, pp. 101–13. For Ellis, *Christos* is the key title.

Meier, J. P. *The Vision of Matthew: Christ, the Church, and Morality in the First Gospel*. New York: Paulist Press, 1978. Offers an alternative structure for Matthew to that of Kingsbury. This analysis is a modified form of Bacon's fivefold structure. Matthew has adjusted salvation history to the Jewish rejection of the Messiah and the consequent broadening of the Christian mission to embrace the Gentiles. Son of God and Son of Man are the key christological titles that fit this restructuring of salvation history.

Davies, W. D. *The Setting of the Sermon on the Mount*. New York and Cambridge: Cambridge University Press, 1964. Despite its title, this work is not restricted to the Sermon on the Mount. It relates Matthew's thought to the emerging Judaism of the post-Jamnia period.

Bornkamm, G.; Barth, G.; and Held, H. J. *Tradition and Interpretation in Matthew*. Philadelphia: Westminster Press, 1963. This is the pioneering redaction-critical study of Matthew, and emphasizes the Law, ecclesiology, and future eschatology as Matthew's main concerns.

Luke

Conzelmann, H. *The Theology of St. Luke*. Eng. trans. G. Buswell. Philadelphia: Fortress Press, 1980; London: Faber & Faber, 1960. A pioneering redaction-critical work on Luke, originally published in German in 1954. The other work, an essay by Edward Lohse, "Lukas als Theologe der Heilsgeschichte," also published in 1954, is better but regrettably has not been translated.

Flender, H. *Luke, Theologian of Redemptive History*. Eng. trans. R. H. Fuller and I. Fuller. Philadelphia: Fortress Press; London: SPCK, 1967. Another redaction-critical study introducing some important modifications to Conzelmann's characterization of the three periods in Luke's pattern of salvation history.

Brown, S. *Apostasy and Perseverance in the Theology of Luke*. Rome: Pontifical Biblical Institute, 1969. Refutes Conzelmann's characterization of the middle period of Jesus' ministry in Luke as a "Satanless time."

Marshall, I. H. *Luke: Historian and Theologian*. Exeter: Paternoster, 1970. A conservative evangelical scholar makes a cautious use of the redaction-critical method in a critique of Conzelmann.

Keck, L. E., and Martyn, J. L., eds. *Studies in Luke-Acts*. 1966. Reprint. Philadelphia: Fortress Press, 1980. Most of the essays are on Acts, but this volume does contain as essay by P. S. Minear, integrating the infancy narrative into Luke's scheme of salvation history, which Conzelmann had omitted to do.

Talbert, C. H., ed. *Perspectives on Luke-Acts*. Perspectives in Religious Studies 5. Danville, Va.: Association of Baptist Professors of Religion,

1978. A collection of essays derived mostly from papers read at the Luke-Acts seminar conducted under the auspices of the Society for Biblical Literature during 1972–78. While none of the essays deals directly with Lukan christology, several bear indirectly on it.

Bovon, F. *Luc le théologien: Vingt-cinq ans de récherches*, 1950–75. Neuchâtel: Delachaux & Niestlé, 1978. For those who know French, this work contains a useful summary of recent work on the christology of Luke-Acts on pp. 131–210.

Fitzmyer, J. A. *The Gospel According to Luke (I–IX)*. AB 28. New York: Doubleday & Co., 1981. Pages 143–283. Fitzmyer prefaces his commentary with a lengthy discussion of all aspects of Lukan theology; pp. 192–231 discuss the two aspects of Luke's picture of Jesus, the Christ-event in itself, and the salvific effects of the Christ-event.

NOTES

1. J. D. Kingsbury, *Matthew: Structure, Christology, Kingdom* (Philadelphia: Fortress Press, 1975), pp. 40–83.

2. Ibid., pp. 7–37.

3. Cf. S. Brown, "The Matthean Community and the Gentile Mission," *NovT* 22 (1980): 193–221, argues that the Matthean *Sitz im Leben* was that the tightening up of Judaism had led the community to turn toward Gentile converts. Matthew seeks to defend this development at a time when it was still controversial.

4. See, e.g., J. P. Meier, *The Vision of Matthew: Christ, the Church, and Morality in the First Gospel* (New York: Paulist Press, 1978), pp. 52–166.

5. W. D. Davies, *The Setting of the Sermon on the Mount* (New York and Cambridge: Cambridge University Press, 1964), pp. 256–315.

6. For the text of the *Birkath ha-minim*, see ibid., p. 275.

7. D. R. A. Hare, *The Theme of Jewish Persecution in the Gospel According to St. Matthew*, SNTSMS 6 (Cambridge: At the University Press, 1967), pp. 196–249.

8. See W. Trilling, *Das wahre Israel: Studien zur Theologie des Matthäus-Evangeliums* (Leipzig: St. Benno Verlag, 1959).

9. See G. Bornkamm, "End-Expectation and Church in Matthew," in *Tradition and Interpretation in Matthew*, ed. G. Bornkamm, G. Barth, and H. J. Held (Philadelphia: Westminster Press, 1963), pp. 15–51; and E. Schweizer, *Matthäus und seine Gemeinde*, SBS 71 (Stuttgart: Katholisches Bibelwerk Verlag, 1974).

10. G. Bornkamm, *Die Vorgeschichte des sogennanten Zweiten Korintherbriefes*, SHAW.PH (Heidelberg: Universitätsverlag, 1961), pp. 24–32.

11. R. E. Brown, *The Birth of the Messiah* (New York: Doubleday & Co., 1977), pp. 112–16.

12. According to H. J. Schoeps, as noted by Davies in *Setting of the Sermon on the Mount*, p. 87.

13. F. Christ, *Jesus Sophia: Die Sophia-Christologie bei den Synoptikern*, ATANT 57 (Zürich: Zwingli, 1970); M. Suggs, *Wisdom, Christology, and the Law in Matthew's Gospel* (Cambridge, Mass.: Harvard University Press, 1970).

14. See the analysis by J. Fitzmyer, *The Gospel According to Luke (I-IX)*, AB 28 (New York: Doubleday & Co., 1981), pp. 171-92. The quotation is from p. 219.

15. H. Conzelmann, *Die Mitte der Zeit* (Tübingen: J. C. B. Mohr [Paul Siebeck], 1954); English translation: *The Theology of St. Luke* (Philadelphia: Fortress Press; London: Faber & Faber, 1960).

16. H. Flender, *St. Luke: Theologian of Redemptive History* (Philadelphia: Fortress Press; London: SPCK, 1967).

17. Conzelmann has been criticized for omitting Luke 1-2 from his scheme (see P. S. Minear, "Luke's Use of the Birth Stories," in *Studies in Luke-Acts*, ed. L. E. Keck and J. L. Martyn [1966; reprint ed., Philadelphia: Fortress Press, 1980], pp. 122-25). I take the birth stories to be Luke's summation of the Old Testament waiting for the fulfillment of the messianic promises.

18. See S. Brown, *Apostasy and Perseverance in the Theology of Luke* (Rome: Pontifical Biblical Institute, 1969).

19. In this study of Luke's use of the christological titles, I am especially indebted to F. Bovon, *Luc le théologien: Vingt-cinq ans de récherches, 1950-75* (Neuchâtel: Delachaux & Niestlé, 1978), pp. 189-210.

20. H. D. Betz, "Jesus as Divine Man," in *Jesus and the Historian: Essays in Honor of Ernest Cadman Colwell*, ed. F. T. Trotter (Philadelphia: Westminster Press, 1968), pp. 114-33.

21. See R. E. Brown, "Jesus and Elisha," *Perspective* 12 (1971): 85-104.

8

Johannine Christology of the Divine Son

The Birth of a Theological Insight

Moving from the synoptics to John is like stepping into a strangely familiar world. The titles and traditions from the synoptic narratives can still be found there, yet they appear in such a different setting that one is not sure whether they have the same meaning any longer. The miracle traditions in John have been subject to the same type of study used to isolate a Markan miracle source. These studies were pursued with much the same intent, to describe the miracles as carriers of a "divine man" christology in which Jesus appears as the carrier of divine power.[1] Yet the Jesus of the whole Johannine narrative would seem to have carried this perception of Jesus to a level beyond that associated with the miracle-worker. Jesus' foreknowledge and sovereignty over all events, especially those of the passion, are constantly asserted. In order to assess this tendency of Johannine narrative, it is necessary to ask what role it plays within the narrative. It appears to be connected with another Johannine theme: Jesus is uniquely Son of God. That insight makes the passion the greatest of Jesus' signs, since it is the true revelation of his glory.[2]

Recently exegesis of the Fourth Gospel has taken a different direction, thanks to the work of J. Louis Martyn and Raymond E. Brown.[3] The diverse traditions found within the Fourth Gospel, such as the "high christology" of the Logos hymn and the Jewish messianic titles that structure the scenes in the second half of chapter 1, are seen as keys to the autobiography of the Johannine community. The Gospel preserves and reinterprets traditions that have come from the various stages of its development.[4] This insight means that the christological traditions in the Gospel have to be seen as taking us from the founding of the community in the 50s C.E. to the time of the Gospel in the 90s.[5]

A brief sketch of the development of the community also shows that christological debates played an important role in its history. The community would have begun with a group of Jewish Christians who found in Jesus the fulfillment of their messianic hopes. Such a christology is reflected in the christological titles that gather Jesus' first disciples in chapter 1. Johannine christology developed away from the mold set by such messianic expectations when a group of Samaritans, with their polemic against the temple and their expectation of a "prophet like Moses," became part of the community (cf. 4:4–42). Johannine Christians come to recognize that Jesus, not Moses, is the source of salvation. The Gospel frequently presents controversies in which Jesus' superiority to Moses is at issue (3:13, 31; 5:20; 6:46; 6:32–35; 7:16, 23). Jesus is presented as the only one to have seen God and as the one who brings the graciousness and truth of the covenant (1:16–18). Johannine Christians found that they could express their understanding of the superiority of Jesus using the images of descent of the divine Word and preexistence. Sometime around 85 C.E., Jewish authorities decided that those who held such beliefs could not continue to be members of the Jewish synagogue. Some appear to have opted to stay within Judaism (12:42). Others were persecuted by Jewish authorities (16:1–4). The severity of the conflict left its mark on the community. The Johannine writings use some of the harshest language about Judaism of any in the New Testament. Rejected by fellow Jews, the Johannine community turned toward the Gentiles. The desire to include them within Jesus' saving power led to the formation of the great universal symbols so evident in the Gospel.[6]

The christology of the Gospel answers charges that are likely to have been raised by the community's opponents. From the beginning of the controversies (chap. 5) through the passion, one charge is repeated over and over again. Jesus blasphemously claims to make himself God (5:18; 8:58–59; 10:33; 19:7). He claims to have powers that belong only to God, sustaining the living and raising the dead (5:21, 25–29). The Gospel narrative suggests that the claims about the divinity of Jesus that fuel its conflicts are realized in the worship Christians give Jesus. The Gospel opens with a hymn to Jesus as divine Word. Its resurrection appearances in Jerusalem reach their climax in Thomas's confession of faith, "My Lord and my God" (20:28). Chapter 9 reads as if it were an autobiography of a person coming to believe in Jesus. The blind man is challenged by the Jewish authorities, who try to convince him that Jesus is a sinner. He is expelled from the synagogue. The episode concludes with two strong christological affirmations. First, the man worships Jesus as Son of Man (9:38). Then Jesus is pictured as the Son of Man pronouncing judgment on his enemies (9:39–41).[7] This judgment is no longer deferred to the parousia, as it was in the confrontation between Jesus and his enemies in Mark 14:62. Failure to believe in the Son of Man present before them represents their condemnation.

The Johannine community has paid a heavy price for its christological insights. To maintain those convictions publicly, which many did not do,[8] would cost some their associations with family and friends, others positions of honor in the community.[9] When we remember the price that Johannine Christians paid for their christological belief, we will not be tempted to think that christology is a matter of idle speculation. The unique christology of the Fourth Gospel, which had come to identify Jesus with God,[10] exacted its price from the community which came to that insight.

The Preexistent Logos

The christological issue is joined from the first words of the Gospel. Though the hymnic material in the prologue (1:1–18) is often compared with the wisdom hymns, it represents a significant advance beyond their insights.[11] None of the wisdom hymns contains the unequivocal statements of preexistence that we find in the Fourth Gospel. Most present Wisdom as the firstborn creature. Here the Logos exists with and as God prior to any creation.[12] Although commentators differ as to the exact verses they attribute to the Johannine hymn, the following verses give a fair consensus: vv. 1–4, 5 or 9ab; 10–11; 12a?; 14a; 14b?; 14c; 16. It describes the creative and redemptive activity of God's Word. The comments the evangelist inserts into the hymnic material make it clear that he understands everything after verse 5 to refer to the redemptive activity of the Word in Jesus.[13] The description of the incarnation in verses 14 and 16 reminds the reader of God's glory dwelling among his people (cf. Joel 3:17; Ezek. 43:7). It suggests that Jesus brings the graciousness and truthfulness of the new covenant. Throughout the Gospel, the evangelist will consistently play on this theme of Jesus' "true glory." Jesus' farewell discourses conclude with his return to the glory he had had with the Father before the world (17:5). The prologue also introduces another important theme in Johannine christology, Jesus' superiority to Moses. Not only does Jesus bring the grace of the covenant, he is also the only one who can reveal God. He, not Moses, is the only one who has seen God. Thus Jesus becomes the sole source of divine revelation.[14]

Scholarly attempts to trace the background of the Johannine prologue are as varied as the sources of Word (Logos) imagery in the Hellenistic world: the Old Testament Word of God; the Logos in the *Corpus Hermeticum* I; the divine Logos of Stoic philosophy; and speculation about the creative divine Logos in the Jewish philosopher Philo of Alexandria. Since Philo also combines speculation about the Word with that about Wisdom, and since wisdom speculation provides the background for images in the prologue like "light" and rejection by "his own," the traditions used by Philo provide the best background to the Johannine prologue. Those who love wisdom are entitled to be called "sons of God." The prologue shows that those who believe in Jesus, the incarnate Word, are to be called "children of God" (v. 12). Until verse 14, the hymn does not say anything that would surprise a Greek-speaking Jew acquainted with the type of speculation we find in Philo.[15]

John 1:14 speaks about incarnation in a way that goes quite beyond anything Jewish traditions would say about the presence of divine glory. It also goes beyond speaking of Jesus as the full manifestation of divine Wisdom in the way that the wisdom hymns elsewhere in the New Testament do. Though this hymn might seem to be the next stage in development beyond those hymns, it makes a quantum leap beyond them. That leap underlies the charges of blasphemy faced by the Johannine church:

They identify God with a particular human being. The evangelist has united the Logos tradition with Son of God christology (v. 18). The combination makes it clear that Jesus is "son" in a unique sense. He is not "Son of God" in the way that other righteous people or the nation of Israel itself might be spoken of as "sons."[16] A similar transformation is found throughout the Gospel. The great symbols for the people of God are focused in Jesus. He is son, shepherd, vine. All these symbols properly belong to Jesus because of his unique relationship to the Father.[17] Verse 18 reminds us of what this unique sonship implies. Jesus is the source of salvation for all who believe. He is the only revelation of God in the world.[18]

Son of Man and the Transformation of Jewish Messianic Titles

Mark used the title Son of Man in contexts that brought out the paradox of Jesus' suffering messiahship. The Fourth Gospel also contains a number of striking Son of Man sayings, some of which appear to have developed traditions similar to those in Mark.[19] John's use of the title seems to have played an important part in his polemic against Judaism.[20] The controversy stories in John follow a pattern that moves from identification of Jesus with a Jewish messianic title through Midrashic discussion about the Old Testament to the assertion that Jesus as Son of Man cannot be defined by such a discussion:[21]

Mosaic Prophet/Messiah	Discussion	Jesus as Son of Man
3:2	3:4,9	3:13,14
6:14	6:30,31	6:35,38,53,62
7:31,40	7:42,52; 8:13	8:12,28
9:17	9:28,29,34	9:35–41

This pattern is already evident in the second half of chapter 1. The collection of messianic titles in that chapter culminates in the vision of the Son of Man with angels descending and ascending on him. Many interpreters point out that the fig tree (v. 48) recalls rabbinic traditions of discussing the Torah under a fig tree. That symbol might represent the Midrashic discussion that comes between the Jewish messianic titles and the recognition that Jesus as

Son of Man transcends the expectations of the Old Testament and their Midrashic interpretation.

Another example of this pattern appears in the third passion prediction (12:31–34). Jesus' identification with the Son of Man is rejected by the crowd on the grounds that the messiah is to remain forever. Jesus does not try to disprove their interpretation, but utters a judgment oracle against them for their disbelief. Mark 14:62 also attached such an edge of condemnation to a saying about the parousia of the Son of Man. For John, Jesus is that Son of Man in his earthly life. Other Son of Man sayings in the Gospel carry that edge of condemnation (cf. 5:27). The judgment is often attached to failure to believe the truth about Jesus. The Son of Man's ascent to heaven represents the judgment of those scandalized by Jesus as bread of life (6:62).[22] Those who refuse to recognize that Jesus is from the Father are condemned by the saying in 8:28. The "hour," the passion, which has been awaited since the beginning of the Gospel (2:4) begins with a solemn announcement that the time for the Son of Man to be glorified has come (13:31–32). Thus John is able to use the Son of Man symbol, with all the overtones it had acquired in earlier Christian traditions, as a counter to attempts to define Jesus in false messianic categories. It serves as a clear indication that divine glory is present in Jesus, who is from the Father. Consequently, judgment is attached to the choice of belief that faces a person in the encounter with him. He is the only revelation of the Father. To see Jesus is to see God (14:9).

Jesus as the Divine "I Am"

Within the narrative, Jesus' identity with God reaches its fullest expression when he pronounces the divine "I Am." These passages are clustered in the controversy with the Jews in chapter 8 (vv. 24, 28, 58). Later, "I Am" is to console the sorrowful disciples in the face of the coming passion (13:19). Jesus' "I Am" not only makes the uniqueness of his relation to the Father clear, it is also the basis of the claim that saving revelation of God can be found only in Jesus.[23]

The consolation implied in 13:19 depends on the Johannine recognition that the "lifting up" of the Son of Man in crucifixion

is also his glorification. It is the true revelation of his divine identity (8:28). This striking reinterpretation of the crucifixion would
seem to require the groundwork of earlier Christian reflection,
such as we find in the Markan passion narrative. John is careful to
insist that Jesus' identification with God is not blasphemous because Jesus is not a human trying to exalt himself to divine status.
He is always the obedient Son, always acting on the commission
given him by the Father. The use of the "I Am" in 8:24, 28 derives from the divine self-predication in the Old Testament. The
Greek version (Septuagint) of Isa.43:10–11 is particularly striking:

> "You are my witnesses and I am a witness," says the Lord God,
> "and the servant whom I have chosen, that you may know and be-
> lieve and understand that I AM. Before me there was no other God,
> and after me there will be none. I am God, and no one saves except
> me." (au. trans.)

Here God acts as his own witness, just as he is called to do in
Jesus' controversy with the Jews (8:13–15). That testimony re-
quires "knowledge and belief" in the divine "I Am" (8:24, 28).
At first, the crowd shows the required response. Many believe in
Jesus, but that belief will quickly be challenged.

The second half of chapter 8 attacks Jewish confidence in descent from Abraham. Other early Christian traditions also reject
the claim that descent from Abraham entitles a person to salvation
(cf. Luke 16:24; Matt. 3:7–10; 8:11–12). John insists that those
who believe in Jesus are free, those who do not are enslaved to sin
and are children not of Abraham but of Satan. The plot to kill
Jesus becomes a contest between God and Satan (8:41–46; cf.
12:31; 14:30; 16:11; 17:15). The countercharge that Jesus is pos-
sessed (cf. Mark 3:22–25) is met with the assertion that Jesus is
not acting for his own glory (vv. 50, 54). John does not end with
such a saying, however, as the pronouncement story in the synoptic tradition does. Instead, he moves to an even bolder claim: The
person who believes in Jesus will never see death (14:21–24;
15:20; 17:6). Johannine christology implies that the believer has
salvation. Unless a person understands that such a claim is
grounded in Jesus' identification with God, his "I Am," one can

only conclude as the crowd does that he is a blasphemous mad-man. The scene ends with that contrast in dramatic terms. The crowd responds to Jesus' "before Abraham was, I Am" with the attempt to execute him. Thus this scene makes clear what is at stake between Johannine Christians and their opponents. Either belief in Jesus is blasphemous, or it is the only way to saving knowledge of God.

Symbolic "I Am" Statements and the Universality of Jesus

"I Am" statements are not only directed toward defense of Johannine christology against the charge of blasphemy, they also serve to express the universality of Jesus so necessary in the com-munity's turn toward the Gentiles. Many of the symbols in the Gospel are so universal that they could belong to a Hellenistic Jew or to a Gentile. The hymn to Jesus as divine Word (Logos) may have originated with Jewish wisdom and Logos speculation, but it could easily be understood by a person familiar with Stoic images of a divine Logos pervading the universe and human souls. Simi-larly, the "I Am" sayings in the Gospel which are followed by symbolic predicates are similar to "I Am" predications common among those who worshiped the Egyptian goddess Isis. Lists of her attributes identified Isis with all manifestations of divinity and proclaimed her the source of all the blessings of human civili-zation. In the second century, Gnostic writings employ two types of "I Am" pronouncements. First, following the Isaiah tradition, the evil, lower god tries to assert that he is the only god. Second, female figures, partially derived from Jewish images of Wisdom, use the "I Am" form of saying to awaken humanity to its true destiny in the higher, light world. Some of their writings include paradoxical "I Am" aretalogies for the heavenly Eve. Such lists demonstrate the superiority of Gnostic revelation to the con-tradictions of the universe. Though some scholars think that the style of Gnostic revelations influenced John, the Gospel shows none of the peculiarities of Gnostic usage. Both evidence the in-fluence of the "I Am" style of revelation in the Hellenistic world.[24]

The impulse toward universalization seems fundamental to the use of the "I Am" proclamation wherever it occurs. The Johannine sayings, which may be rooted in liturgical symbols,[25] take symbols with Old Testament roots—bread, life, gate, shepherd, resurrection (life), way, truth—which are universal. Christians from diverse backgrounds can use them to join together in affirming that Jesus is savior of all.[26] At the same time, the Johannine tradition maintains the exclusivity of revelation in Jesus. Whatever tradition or symbol a person identifies with the divine, Jesus represents the truth of that symbol. Most of the paradoxes about Jesus' identity with the Father are created by John's use of Jewish symbols and categories in unusual ways. Such paradoxes might not be as striking to a non-Jewish audience as they would be to a Jewish one. However, a pagan audience would be surprised at the combination of a particular human being with the divine claim to "I Am," with the claim to be the exclusive source of revelation (= salvation).[27] Isis may be universal and the truth behind other expressions of the divine, but she neither identifies with a particular human being who dies nor insists that hers is the only way of salvation. It is not surprising that the disputes among Johannine Christians in the next generation show a tendency to dissolve the tension by focusing on the divinity of Jesus and the perfection of the Christian to the exclusion of his humanity and his role as mediator of forgiveness.[28]

Summary

The christology of the Fourth Gospel is closely linked to the changes in the Johannine community and its efforts to reinterpret the traditions it inherited in light of those new experiences. The Gospel shows how a particular group of Christians came to confess the unity of Jesus and God with a clarity unparalleled in the New Testament. Their understanding does not come out of the clear blue sky, however. It has developed the insights of earlier Christian traditions. Now the choice has become inescapable: either Jesus or Moses. John's Jewish opponents appear to have used all the resources of argument at their disposal. They claimed to have the authority of Scripture and tradition on their side. Those who chose Jesus had to pay a high personal price, if not in personal suffering, at least in disrupted relationships with family and friends. Surely John is right: Only God can demand that a person make such a choice. Only God can guarantee that the choice of faith in Jesus over the traditions of Moses means salvation.

Almost every passage in John has implications for christology and soteriology. The issues are presented in the prologue. Christ is the divine Logos. The history of Jesus is the history of the Word. Consequently, his revelation supersedes all others. There is no way to salvation except through the Son, who reveals the Father. The themes of the prologue are fundamental to the presentation of Jesus in the Gospel. He encounters people as Son of Man, who is not bound to any of the categories of messianic speculation. He is present with both divine glory and salvation and with divine judgment against failure to believe his word about the Father.

The most striking assertions of Jesus' unity with the Father come in the divine "I Am" statements. They leave no doubt that Jesus' word is to be accepted as God's Word, since it is pronounced by the Son who is one with the Father. This divine "I Am" is also the basis of salvation. As the true revelation of God, Jesus is Savior of all humanity. He is not just a Jewish teacher who ran into difficulties with his own people. He has conquered Satan and has brought God's salvation to all who believe in him.

Finally, John has not explained the "how" of Jesus' extraordinary relationship with the Father. He has simply and unmistakably set out the terms in which the relationship should be discussed. Jesus is one with the Father and is the son sent by him. He is "only begotten God" (1:18) and "Word became flesh" (1:14). He is divine and also a real human person, who died and was buried like others. Much of the debate about christology in the following centuries attempts to articulate in conceptual terms the vision of Jesus which John has presented in symbolic ones. The tenacity and personal cost with which the Johannine community hung onto its conviction about Jesus should remind us that christology was not idle speculation. It made a difference—the difference between life and death.

FOR FURTHER READING

Brown, R. E. *The Community of the Beloved Disciple*. New York: Paulist Press, 1979. The best introduction to contemporary Johannine studies available. Brown paints a comprehensive picture of the development of Johannine christology from its origin in Jewish-Christian messianic titles through to the "high christology" of the Gospel and epistles which confessed Jesus as God.

All the following commentaries on John contain lengthly discussions of the Logos christology:

Barrett, C. K. *The Gospel According to St. John*. 2d ed. Philadelphia: Westminster Press, 1978.

Brown, R. E. *The Gospel According to John I–XII*. AB 29A. Garden City, N.Y.: Doubleday & Co., 1966.

Schnackenburg, R. *The Gospel According to St. John*. Volume 1. New York: Crossroad, 1968.

Fortna, R. "Christology in the Fourth Gospel: Redaction-Critical Perspectives." *NTS* 21 (1974–75): 489–504. Fortna applies redaction-critical methods to show the development of Son of God christology in the Fourth Gospel.

———. "Source and Redaction in the Fourth Gospel's Portrayal of Jesus' Signs." *JBL* 89 (1970): 151–66. An example of the method of isolating the "signs source" used by the evangelist.

Martyn, J. L. *History and Theology in the Fourth Gospel*. Rev. ed. Nashville: Abingdon Press, 1979. Revision of Martyn's 1967 work, which turned the attention of Johannine scholarship to the situation of the Johannine community as it is reflected in the Gospel. The christology of the Gospel can be seen as developed over against the Jewish community which had driven Christians out of the synagogue. At the same time, the reaction of Judaism had been provoked by the Johannine claims for Jesus.

MacRae, G. W. "The Fourth Gospel and Religionsgeschichte." *CBQ* 32 (1970): 13–24. MacRae describes the universalizing thrust of Johannine symbols. They make it possible for Christians of diverse religious backgrounds to find salvation in Jesus.

Meeks, W. "The Man from Heaven in Johannine Sectarianism." *JBL* 91 (1972): 44–72. Meeks applies contemporary anthropological and sociological insights to the dualistic symbols of the Fourth Gospel. He suggests that they reflect the community's isolation from its environment. At the same time, use of such symbols may also increase such isolationist tendencies within the community. Consequently, the Gospel lent itself to Gnostic, sectarian interpretation in the second century.

NOTES

1. See the treatments of the Johannine "signs source" in R. Fortna, *The Gospel of Signs* (New York and Cambridge: Cambridge University Press, 1970); idem, "Source and Redaction in the Fourth Gospel's Portrayal of Jesus' Signs," *JBL* 89 (1970): 151–66; W. Nicol, *The Semeia in the Fourth Gospel* (Leiden: E. J. Brill, 1972).

2. See R. Fortna, "Christology in the Fourth Gospel: Redaction-Critical Perspectives," *NTS* 21 (1974–75): 489–504. G. W. E. Nickelsburg ("The Genre and Function of the Markan Passion Narrative," *HTR* 73 [1980]) thinks that the pre-Markan passion narrative may have already developed the theme of exaltation from the cross out of the genre of vindication of the righteous (pp. 179–80).

3. See J. L. Martyn, *History and Theology in the Fourth Gospel*, 2d ed. (Nashville: Abingdon Press, 1979); and R. E. Brown, *The Community of the Beloved Disciple* (New York: Paulist Press, 1979).

4. Brown, *Community of the Beloved Disciple*, pp. 52–58.

5. The First Epistle of John provides insight into the christological disputes among Johannine Christians at the end of the century; see ibid., pp. 103–44. However, 1 John continues to use the christological slogans of the earlier period against his opponents; see P. Perkins, *The Johannine Epistles* (Wilmington, Del.: Michael Glazier, 1979). Thus, the christology of the Johannine community is fixed by the Gospel.

6. Brown, *Community of the Beloved Disciple*, pp. 27–58.

7. Ibid., pp. 48–51.

8. See Brown's discussion of those who were "crypto-Christians," ibid., pp. 71–73.

9. Honor was not something that a person in ancient society would readily give up; see Peter Brown, *The Making of Late Antiquity* (Cambridge, Mass.: Harvard University Press, 1978), pp. 21–45.

10. Sometimes John suggests equality between Son and Father, while at other times the Son appears to be subordinate; see Brown, *Community of the Beloved Disciple*, pp. 53–54.

11. See ibid., pp. 45–46, and J. D. G. Dunn, *Christology in the Making: A New Testament Inquiry into the Origins of the Doctrine of the Incarnation* (Philadelphia: Westminster Press, 1980), p. 239.

12. Even those exegetes who deny that the prologue contains a pre-Johannine hymn admit that its themes support the combination of divine and human which emerges in the account of Jesus' ministry; for example, see C. K. Barrett, *The Gospel According to St. John*, 2d ed. (Philadelphia: Westminster Press, 1978), pp. 149–70. Barrett comments, "John intends the whole of his gospel to be read in the light of verse 1. The words and deeds of Jesus are those of God; if this is not true, the book is blasphemous" (p. 156).

13. Some interpreters think that the middle verses originally referred to the activity of the Word prior to the incarnation.

14. See P. Perkins, *The Gospel According to John* (Chicago: Franciscan Herald Press, 1978), pp. 3–9.

15. Dunn, *Christology in the Making*, pp. 215–42.

16. Ibid., p. 244.

17. Perkins, *Gospel According to John*, pp. 171–72; R. Schnackenburg, *The Gospel According to St. John* (New York: Crossroad, 1980), 2:172–86.

18. Schnackenburg, *Gospel According to St. John*, pp. 185–86; T. Forestell, *The Word of the Cross: Salvation as Revelation in the Fourth Gospel* (Rome: Pontifical Biblical Institute, 1974), pp. 37–41.

19. Cf. John 1:51 / / Mark 14:62; John 5:27 / / Mark 2:10; John 12:34 (cf. 3:14) / / Mark 8:31; so N. Perrin, *A Modern Pilgrimage in New Testament Christology* (Philadelphia: Fortress Press, 1974), pp. 120–21; also R. G. Hammerton-Kelly, *Pre-existence, Wisdom, and the Son of Man*, SNTSMS (New York and Cambridge: Cambridge University Press, 1973), pp. 224–41.

20. Brown, *Community of the Beloved Disciple*, pp. 73–81, suggests that John may also be opposing inadequate faith in Jesus among Jewish Christians.

21. Martyn, *History and Theology in the Fourth Gospel*, pp. 130–35.

22. Brown, *Community of the Beloved Disciple*, pp. 74, 82–83, suggests that the Jewish Christians whose faith is inadequate may be represented by the "Disciples" who leave Jesus because they are offended by his presentation of the Eucharist.

23. Schnackenburg, *Gospel According to St. John*, pp. 79–89.

24. Perkins, *Gospel According to John*, pp. 103–5.

25. Schnackenburg, *Gospel According to St. John*, pp. 79–81.

26. See G. W. MacRae, "The Fourth Gospel and Religionsgeschichte," *CBQ* 32 (1970): 13–24.

27. And also some other Christians, if Brown's suggestion that John also opposes Jewish Christians is correct.

28. Brown, *Community of the Beloved Disciple*, pp. 109–35.

9

The Crucified God

The Cross and the Historical Jesus

What place did the cross have in Jesus' own self-understanding and sense of mission? Rudolf Bultmann, as is well known, was skeptical on this score. All we know, he maintained, is that Jesus was crucified as a messianic pretender, as irrational an end as Camus's death on a motorcycle. We know nothing of his intention with respect to the cross. That intention is irrelevant, anyhow, for assuming we could discover it, it would then deprive faith of its quality as decision. That decision can come only in face of the kerygma. Yet the kerygma proclaims the cross as the saving event.[1] Can we be satisfied with pure proclamation, without any historical basis? After all, there were many crosses in first-century Palestine. Why did the kerygma pick on this particular one? Unless we can answer that question, the kerygma becomes a myth erected on the basis of a mathematical point (Jesus' death) without any shape or dimension.

It was this worry about kerygmatic docetism that led to the so-called new quest of the historical Jesus.[2] On the negative side, the new quest refused to build anything on the passion predictions of the synoptics. These were critically suspect for at least three reasons: (1) they share the whole problematic of the Son of Man title; (2) they are clearly *vaticinia ex eventu* (prophecies after the event), reflecting a knowledge of the passion narratives and couched in their language; (3) they presuppose a No-Yes *theologia crucis* of the early kerygma (the cross as Israel's rejection of Jesus, the resurrection as God's vindication of him). Negative, too, was their attitude to bread and cup words in the accounts of the Last Supper. These represent a developing liturgical catechesis[3] of the post-Easter communities and even an etiological cult myth. Mark 10:45b is derived from the same creative milieu.

On the positive side, Jesus' baptism involved from the very start of his ministry an identification with the sinner. This identification continued to be expressed in Jesus' eating with the outcast and in the meals at which he served his disciples. Jesus interpreted his conduct in sayings and parables as the bringing of eschatological salvation to sinners. Jesus' understanding of his conduct was expressed in terms of what God was doing through him, that is, a theology of Jesus. This answers the problem that earlier scholars raised about the parable of the prodigal son. Where is Jesus in that parable?[4] Does that parable mean God can forgive sinners without the necessity of the cross? The answer is that God does so precisely through the obedient activity of Jesus. So one cannot play off the parables against the cross.

Then Jesus journeys to Jerusalem. Not in order to die, however, for that might imply pathological suicide tendencies.[5] Rather, it was to continue his eschatological message with its offer of salvation (and judgment) at the heart of Israel's community and religious life. And the outcome was inevitable, if not directly sought. Did Jesus envisage the outcome? As Ernst Fuchs and others have pointed out[6] he had the example of John the Baptist to go by; since the Maccabees, martyrdom had been regarded as an inseparable part of the prophetic vocation. That Jesus explicitly envisaged this possible outcome is indicated by the logion, Luke 13:31–32, which as critically reconstructed[7] reads: "Behold, I cast out demons and perform cures today and tomorrow. . . . Nevertheless I must go on my way . . . the day following; for it cannot be that a prophet should perish away from Jerusalem." Finally, even if the bread and cup words at the Last Supper are critically suspect, the supper tradition contains three logia whose claim to authenticity is high and which throw significant light on Jesus' attitude to his impending death. The first is the covenant saying, Luke 22:29, a saying that led to the subsequent expansion of the cup word in different forms in the Markan and Pauline-Lukan tradition, thus indicating that at this point the cup word is rooted in the authentic Jesus tradition. The second logion is the service saying, which has triple attestation (Luke 22:27; John

13:1–20; Mark 10:45a). This logion probably originated in the Supper tradition, and in Mark it has attracted to itself the ransom saying (v. 45b), also derived from the developing tradition of the cup word. The third logion is the eschatological saying at the Supper, doubly attested from Mark (14:25) and from the special Lukan tradition (Luke 22:16, 18), surviving in an attenuated form in 1 Cor. 11:26 ("until he comes") and in John 6:40 ("I will raise him up at the last day"), and further supported by Jesus' parables and sayings about the eschatological banquet. These three sayings put together support the view that Jesus regarded his death as of a piece with his previous ministry. It was the culmination of his self-giving service in bringing the eschatological salvation to his followers and the decisive event which would lead to the coming of the kingdom and the establishment of the eschatological covenant.

The Death of Christ in the
Post-Easter Kerygma

Initially, as we have already noted, the death of Jesus was seen to be the rejection of his offer of salvation on the part of his contemporaries, while the resurrection was seen as God's vindication of him and the consequent renewal of that offer. The death as such was not yet viewed as a salvific act of God in its own right. The latter interpretation emerges first in what is perhaps a slightly later form of the kerygma, found in a catechetical-kerygmatic tradition in 1 Cor. 15:3. Here we have *hyper*-language ("Christ died *for* our sins") applied for the first time to Jesus' death. The same language appears in the bread and cup words in the eucharistic tradition, where it appears to be an expansion of an earlier original without it, and in Mark 10:45b, which is probably also of eucharistic origin, like the service logion to which it has been attached.[8] The origin of this *hyper*-language is in dispute. Some have sought its origin in the martyr ideology of post-Maccabean Judaism.[9] I have elsewhere proposed an origin in the paschal liturgy, perhaps from the first Christian celebration of the Passover after Jesus' death.[10] In any case, Isa. 53:11–12 seems to have been the source of the *hyper*-language. Once this step was taken, other Old Testament themes contributed toward the development, notably the covenant-blood motif from Exod. 24:8 and Zech. 9:11, and the paschal lamb motif (1 Cor. 5:7–8).

Paul's Theologia Crucis

Paul took over from his predecessors the kerygmatic (1 Cor. 15:3–8) and the liturgical (1 Cor. 11:23–25) catecheses. Wherever Paul uses *hyper-*, or blood, language, we may assume that it is derived from these pre-Pauline formulas. To a greater degree than the earliest kerygma, Paul made the death of Christ central (Gal. 3:1; 1 Cor. 1:23; cf. 1 Cor. 2:2). This does not mean that he did not also preach the resurrection (e.g., 1 Cor. 15:14), but it does mean, in Eberhardt Güttgemann's expressive phrase, that the resurrection did not relegate the cross to the archives. Rather, the resurrection as well as anticipating the end also made the cross as salvation event ever present in the kerygma and in sacramental celebrations.

We will now seek to penetrate more deeply into Paul's theology of the cross by examining some of his salient texts. In Gal. 2:20 he writes: "the Son of God, who loved me and gave himself for me." Here, in contrast to other formulas, the subject is Christ rather than God—but not Christ over against God, as though Christ loved us whereas God was only angry with us. Christ's love and God's love veritably coincide: "God shows *his* love for us in that . . . Christ died for us" (Rom. 5:8). Second, the love of God in these texts is not an abstract idea but a concrete event, the event of Christ's death on the cross. Third, Paul takes the *paradidonai* (self-giving) language from the tradition and proceeds to individualize it: who gave himself *for me*.

In Gal. 3:13 Paul writes: "Christ redeemed us from the curse of the law, having become a curse for us." He goes on to elucidate this statement by an appeal to Deut. 27:26, "Cursed be every one who hangs on a tree." It has been suggested that the source of this bold notion is the Jewish attacks on the Christian message made prior to Paul. Jesus could not be the messiah because he died on a tree and was therefore accursed according to the Deuteronomy text. There may be echoes of this attack in the use of "tree" in the early kerygma (Acts 5:30; 10:39; 13:29). Far from denying it, the early church gloried in the fact that Jesus underwent this accursed death. Paul reflects further on the idea and couples it with another text about a curse: "Cursed be every one who does not abide by all things written in the book of the law, and do them" (Gal. 3:10). As Paul explains in Rom. 3:22, all have sinned. In other words, Christ in his death on the cross submitted to the curse under which all humanity lies. As Ernst Käsemann has put it, Christ entered into our banishment from God's covenant. Christ entered into our human plight, our existence under sin which separates us from God. This does not mean, as in later evangelicalism, that Jesus sustained God's anger, that Yahweh's rod fell upon Christ as the only acceptable victim and so achieved satisfaction. Rather, there is a complete unity of will between God and Christ: "In Christ God was reconciling the world to himself" (2 Cor. 5:19). In the person of his Son, God enters the bitterest consequence of human sin, namely, the curse it entails. Does this mean, as much evangelical teaching has claimed, that God in the person of his Son suffers (and propitiates) his own wrath? Paul would never have said this. When he speaks of the "wrath" of God, as in Rom. 1:16–18, he is speaking of God's eschatological judgment against evil. The cross is an eschatological event challenging that judgment and therefore can be said to reveal the wrath of God which is God's judgment. But to speak of an individual, even of Jesus, as under that wrath is to move beyond the linguistic framework of the apocalyptic concept of the day of the Lord, which is behind the concept of divine wrath. Thus the question raised by much evangelical theology at this point cannot even be articulated within the theological framework Paul is using.[11]

There is a passage of similar import in 2 Cor. 5:21: "[God] made [Jesus Christ] to be sin on our behalf." (au. trans.). The best interpretation of this difficult verse is that God put Christ in the place of sinners, that is, in the state of alienation from God which is the consequence of human sin. Once again, evangelicals have used this passage as the basis of a doctrine of penal substitution. But here again we must be cautious. Paul is not talking about punishment in the juridical sense, as in Anselm's doctrine of satisfaction. He is not thinking in quantitative terms—so much sin, so much punishment, sustained in full by an innocent victim.

Paul is thinking rather of an existential relationship between God and sinners which Christ enters and transforms.

We come now to Rom. 3:25–26. Since Bultmann, this text has been widely regarded as a pre-Pauline formula with Pauline glosses. The hymn reads as follows (with glosses in parentheses):

> whom God put forward as an expiation by his blood (to be received by faith), because in his divine forbearance he had passed over former sins; (it was to prove at the present time that he himself is righteous and that he justifies him who has faith in Jesus).

Paul is responsible for adding the material concerning faith and justification. Note again that it is God who takes the initiative: God "put him forward." Once again, there is no dichotomy between God and Christ. But the major problem is the translation of *hilastērion*. The Revised Standard Version and the New English Bible, following C. H. Dodd,[12] translate it "expiation." This means God's act is wiping sin away. The Vulgate, followed by the King James Version, translated it *"propitiationem,"* and conservative evangelicals, following medieval theology once more, insist on taking it thus.[13] "Propitiation" implies that man is the subject and God is the object. Man does something to appease God's anger. This fits in with the doctrines of satisfaction and penal substitution. Anders Nygren has proposed a third translation,[14] namely, mercy seat (Heb. *kapporeth*). The "mercy seat" in the temple was sprinkled with blood on the Day of Atonement. Here it could mean that God made Jesus the place of atonement. Eduard Lohse, however, has marshaled several arguments against this interpretation.[15] The context nowhere suggests that Jesus is a new *kapporeth*. The Old Testament always uses the article with the noun, but Paul has no article. "Put forward" suggests a public display, whereas the mercy seat was located behind the veil. The blood of Jesus is always sprinkled on the sinner, never on a cult object. These are weighty arguments. The choice is probably between propitiation and expiation. I have argued elsewhere that while the pre-Pauline formula certainly meant "expiation," Paul's thought is moving toward the meaning "propitiation."[16] As C. K. Barrett has remarked,[17] "It would be wrong to neglect the fact that expiation has as it were the effect of propitiation."

The Crucified God—Systematic
Considerations

But can we call Christ a crucified God? Certainly Paul says that Christ suffered, and in that Christ suffered God acted. It was, as we have seen, an act of love on the part of both God and Christ. No distinction can be drawn between the act of the Father and the act of the Son. They are one and the same in execution and in effect. If Christ suffered, did God then suffer too?

In the patristic period, the Monarchians and Sabellians suggested that on the cross God suffered. This was the heresy of Patripassianism and was repudiated by the Catholic church because of the tenaciously held Greek view of the impassibility of God. In the trenches in World War I the Anglican army chaplain Studdart Kennedy ("Woodbine Willie") revived the notion to cope with the mud and blood of Flanders, attacking the impassibility of God in his poems and defending Patripassianism in his prose writings. More recently, the death-of-God theology took up from Friedrich Nietzsche the slogan "God is dead" in a negative sense to denote the abandonment of faith in a transcendent reality. The cross was taken as the symbol of this, and its consequence was an exclusive affirmation of God's immanence in humanity.

Both Catholic (Karl Rahner) and Protestant (Jürgen Moltmann) theologians took up the notion of a crucified God in a positive sense.[18] They found in the concept a way to speak about the meaning of the cross in itself prior to its saving effect on us. They find a basis for this in the kenosis passage (Phil. 2:6–11), which discloses the meaning of the cross within the being of God. God became man in Christ and suffered death and dereliction. Here was the supreme expression of his self-giving love.

Such a theology of the crucified God requires evaluation in the light of both Scripture and the church's later dogma. Is it tenable? As far as Scripture is concerned, it goes beyond what Paul said. As we have seen, for Paul God was at work in the death of his Son, but only the Son suffered and died. Paul had not yet arrived at the point of saying that the Son as well as the Father is truly God, although his thought was moving in that direction. He thought in

terms of a unity of will and a unity of effect, rather than in terms
of a unity of being. But the Fourth Gospel, as we have also seen,
went further in projecting the Father-Son relationship from the
earthly ministry to a preincarnation eternity. If we are prepared to
grant that the Fourth Gospel, led by the Spirit of truth, was enabled to penetrate the depths of Jesus' *Abba*-experience, if it
rightly understood that experience as a disclosure not just of a
relationship between the human Jesus and God but between two
aspects of the being of God himself, the Father aspect and the Son
aspect, then we must infer that the Son aspect of God was directly
involved in the suffering and death of the cross, not just indirectly
like the Father, as Paul already saw.

But how are we to relate the humanity of Jesus to this aspect of
God's being which is incarnate in him? Chalcedonian orthodoxy,
with its doctrine of two natures, could only assert that the human
nature, not the divine nature, died; and if it spoke of the crucified
God or the death of God, it could do so only under the principle of
communicatio idiomatum (what is predicated by the humanity is by
transference predicated also of the divinity, as in Mary's title
Theotokos, Godbearer). But what if we pursue a christology from
below? Building on the historical Jesus' *Abba*-experience and its
development in Johannine thought, we can perhaps say that in the
cross of Jesus, as articulated in the Markan *Eloi, Eloi, lama
sabachtani?* we penetrate into the mystery of the relationship not
only between the man Jesus and God, but also between the divine
Son and the Father. In the moment of the cross, the Father sur-
renders the Son to death, the Son who in the totality of his human
person is the revelation not only of the Father but also of that
other aspect within the being of God which theologians following
the New Testament call the Son. If this were otherwise, then we
would have to say that there is one part of Jesus' being which is
separable from his humanity and which does not die. The whole
person of Jesus died on the cross, and in the totality of his human
person (not just some part of it) he was the definitive revelation of
God, not only of God the Father but also of God the Son, which he
was. Further, it is out of this mysterious transaction between the
Father and the Son that the Spirit is bestowed upon the believers
(John 19:30). Hence the doctrine of the Trinity, like christology,

is a doctrine not merely from above but also from below. We affirm the Trinity, like the divine Sonship of Jesus, because of what we have experienced in the cross. This may be why from ancient times baptism in the threefold name was accomplished with the sign of the cross, and why Christians have traditionally signed themselves with the cross as they say, "In the name of the Father and of the Son and of the Holy Spirit."

Summary

Jesus did not interpret his death as such as the saving event, but he did see in it the culmination of his eschatological mission and therefore of his offer of salvation. After Easter, this offer was vindicated and renewed, and the Passover celebration led to the kerygmatic affirmation: Christ died *for our sins*.

Paul developed a soteriology on the basis of this kerygma. In the cross, Christ entered fully into our human plight, including our alienation from God, the bitterest consequence of sin, and so overcame it. This was an act of self-giving love in which the Father was involved as well as the Son. But as far as Paul could see, the deity of God was only indirectly involved: He sent the Son and gave the Son, and the Son perfectly obeyed his Father's will, so that the cross was also the act of the Father. But Paul could not yet speak of a crucified God or of the death of God, however much he was feeling his way toward this, for example, by his addition of "even death on a cross" to the pre-Pauline hymn (Phil. 2:8).

In the dogmatic developments after the New Testament period, the church's thinking was dominated by the Greek conception of the impassibility of God. Hence, when the deity and humanity of the incarnate Son were affirmed at Chalcedon, it could speak of the crucified God or of the death of God only by appealing to the principle of the *communicatio idiomatum*. Strictly speaking, only the human nature died; the divine nature could not die.

We finally suggested a new approach to the concepts of the crucified God and the death of God from the perspective of a christology from below. Johannine thought projected the Father/Son relationship disclosed in Jesus' *Abba*-experience back to the life of God in eternity before the incarnation. Subsequent reflection has combined the Johannine insight with the Markan cry of dereliction on the cross to see in the cross the supreme revelation of the eternal relationship between the Father and the Son (as well as of the inner relationship between the persons of the Trinity).

Thus we are compelled to acknowledge that the death of Jesus as well as his whole previous life was the definitive revelation and action of God going out of himself in self-giving love. In this way a christology from below can speak, cautiously, of a crucified God or of the death of God, not merely by means of the *communicatio idiomatum* as in christology from above, but as a profound expression of the depth of God's involvement in the cross.

FOR FURTHER READING

Schweizer, E. *Jesus.* Eng. trans. D. E. Green. Richmond: John Knox Press, 1971. Not a life of Jesus, but almost a theology of the New Testament from a christological perspective, covering the historical Jesus, the early church, the gospels, and the epistolary literature.

Knox, J. *The Death of Christ.* Nashville: Abingdon Press, 1958. Notable for its insistence that Jesus could not have gone up to Jerusalem deliberately in order to die. Lays great emphasis on the remembered experience of the Christian community as the source of its doctrine.

Hengel, M. *The Atonement: The Origins of the Doctrine in the New Testament.* Eng. trans. J. Bowden. Philadelphia: Fortress Press; London: SCM Press, 1981. Argues against a later origin of the doctrine of atonement, finding its roots in the earliest church, even in the sayings of Jesus. Notable in its treatment of "dying for" in classical antiquity.

Morris, L. *The Apostolic Preaching of the Cross.* London: Tyndale Press, 1955. A scholarly, conservative evangelical treatment of New Testament soteriology, defending the positions of Protestant scholasticism.

Rahner, K. *Theological Investigations.* Volume 4. New York: Seabury Press; London: Darton, Longman & Todd, 1966. Pages 105–20.

Moltmann, J. *The Crucified God.* New York: Harper & Row, 1974; London: SCM Press, 1975. These two works by Rahner and Moltmann represent respectively a Catholic and a Protestant response to the death-of-God theology of the 1960s. Both seek to move beyond the *communicatio idiomatum* of a crucified God, finding in the cross a revelation of a dynamic transaction within the life of the tri-une God himself.

Hoskyns, E. C., and Davey, F. N. *Crucifixion-Resurrection.* Edited by G. S. Wakefield. London: SPCK, 1981. The bulk of this work was written in the 1930s as a theological sequel to *Riddle of the New Testament* (London: Faber & Faber, 1931) and was published after the deaths of both authors. While incomplete and in many ways dated, it is a powerful statement of the central themes of New Testament theology.

NOTES

1. For a fuller treatment of New Testament soteriology, see R. H. Fuller, "Jesus Christ as Savior in the New Testament," *Int.* 35 (1981): 145–56.

2. A history of its early stages is provided in J. M. Robinson, *A New Quest of the Historical Jesus*, SBT 25 (Naperville, Ill.: Alec R. Allenson, 1959). The developments since 1960 are covered by G. Aulén, *Jesus in Contemporary Historical Research* (Philadelphia: Fortress Press, 1976).

3. Protestant scholars, especially German Lutherans, frequently refer to 1 Cor. 11:23–25 as an actual liturgical formula. This is an anachronism. Liturgical history indicates that the words of institution were not an invariable part of the liturgy in early times and that they were not regarded as consecratory until the Western Middle Ages. Nor did they become the sole content of the eucharistic prayer until the Reformation. Rather, the institution narrative forms an agenda or catechesis, describing the actions of the liturgy.

4. The question was asked by E. Schweizer in his *Jesus* (Richmond: John Knox Press, 1971), but he proceeded to give a positive answer. H. Rashdall, *The Idea of Atonement in Christian Theology* (London: Macmillan & Co., 1919), typically played off the "simple teaching" of the parable of the prodigal son against the elaborate abstractions of the Pauline doctrine of the atonement.

5. J. Knox, *The Death of Christ* (Nashville: Abingdon Press, 1958), pp. 72–73.

6. E. Fuchs, *Studies of the Historical Jesus*, SBT 42 (Naperville, Ill.: Alec Allenson, 1960), p. 26.

7. I adopted Wellhausen's reconstruction of this logion in my earliest book, R. H. Fuller, *The Mission and Achievement of Jesus*, SBT 12 (London: SCM Press, 1954), pp. 62–63. It was gratifying to find G. Bornkamm, *Jesus of Nazareth* (New York: Harper & Row, 1956), pp. 154 and 210, n. 2, making use of Wellhausen's reconstruction for the same purpose.

8. Despite the recent claim of M. Hengel, *The Atonement: A Study of the Origins of the Doctrine of the New Testament* (Philadelphia: Fortress Press, 1981), pp. 71–73, followed by P. Stuhlmacher, that Mark 10:45b is an authentic Jesus logion spoken at the Last Supper, I still follow N. Perrin, *A Modern Pilgrimage In New Testament Christology* (Philadelphia: Fortress Press, 1974), pp. 118–19, in accepting a post-Easter origin for

it. Its absence from Luke 22:27 tells heavily against its authenticity to Jesus.

9. C. K. Barrett, "The Background of Mark 10:45," in *New Testament Essays: Studies in Honour of T. W. Manson*, ed. A. J. B. Higgins (Manchester, Eng.: Manchester University Press, 1959), pp. 11–14.

10. R. H. Fuller, "The Double Origin of the Eucharist," *BR* 8 (1963): 60–72, esp. pp. 71–72.

11. For a statement of the evangelical doctrine questioned here, see G. E. Ladd, *A Theology of the New Testament* (Grand Rapids: Wm. B. Eerdmans, 1974), pp. 430–34. For the apocalyptic framework of Paul's thought, see J. C. Beker, *Paul the Apostle: The Triumph of God in Life and Thought* (Philadelphia: Fortress Press, 1980).

12. C. H. Dodd, *The Bible and the Greeks* (London: Hodder & Stoughton, 1935), pp. 82–95.

13. Leon Morris, "The Meaning of *Hilastērion* in Romans iii.25," *NTS* 2 (1955): 33–43; also idem, *The Apostolic Preaching of the Cross* (London: Tyndale Press, 1955), pp. 125–85; Ladd, *Theology of the New Testament*, pp. 429–33.

14. Anders Nygren, *Commentary on Romans* (Philadelphia: Fortress Press, 1949), pp. 156–58.

15. E. Lohse, *Martyrer und Gottesknecht* (Göttingen: Vandenhoeck & Ruprecht, 1955), pp. 151–52.

16. R. H. Fuller, "Jesus Christ as Savior in the New Testament," *Int* 35 (1981): 145–56, esp. 149–50.

17. C. K. Barrett, *A Commentary on the Epistle to the Romans*, HNTC (New York: Harper & Brothers, 1957), p. 78.

18. Karl Rahner, "On the Theology of the Incarnation," *Theological Investigations*, vol. 4 (New York: Seabury Press; London: Darton, Longman & Todd, 1966), pp. 105–20; idem, *The Concise Sacramentum Mundi* (New York: Seabury Press, 1975), p. 770; Jürgen Moltmann, *The Crucified God* (New York: Harper & Row, 1974; London: SCM Press, 1975).

10

From the New Testament to Chalcedon

The Shift Within the New Testament

Our explorations into the christology of the New Testament have shown that there was a perceptible shift of focus between the earliest kerygma and the developed Johannine christology, the latest development recorded in the New Testament. The earliest christology was focused on the soteriological work of Christ, particularly on his death and resurrection, though also including at times what went before (his early ministry) and what came after (his exaltation and his coming again). Without intending it, the sending formula began to shift the focus from the end of Christ's earthly way to the beginning, from his leaving the world to his entry into it. In itself, this was not a shift away from salvation history, for the sending christology was rooted in the prophetic notion of God's election of individuals to play a significant role in history, often at the moment of birth or conception.

A parallel movement, and one much more far-reaching in its consequences, was the identification of Jesus with God's Wisdom and the consequent development of a preexistence-incarnation christology. As we see in the christological hymns, this too was not originally a departure from the salvation-historical perspective. The early Christians experienced the Christ event as a *recognition* of One already known, not just as a first-time disclosure. The God who was revealing himself in the Christ event was the same God who had been active all along in Israel's salvation history. And behind that was the general experience of humanity, its moral sensitivity and dependence on the transcendent. Further back, too, was the experience of creation as an act of God's self-communication. A way to relate the Christ event to these prior experiences was discovered in the wisdom and Logos traditions of Hellenistic Judaism.[1] The christological hymns, read in the light of the later dogmatic tradition, appear to pursue a christology from above, but this is not so. They really start not with what the preexistent redeemer was before his historical existence but with their experience of the Christ event. Then they attempt to relate that experience to their previous experiences of God. The procedure is analogous to the way the Exodus narrative came eventually to be prefaced by creation stories in the Pentateuch.

The Johannine school took the next step of combining this christology with a profound meditation on the significance of Jesus' *Abba*-experience, which projected Jesus' Father/Son relationship onto the preincarnate life of the Logos, thus equating the two images, Son and Logos. Further, by placing the Logos hymn at the beginning of the Gospel, before the earthly history of Jesus, it unintentionally gave an impetus to the doing of christology from above. The story now read this way: The preexistent Logos, who shared the very being with God, became flesh, or took upon himself our human nature. This posed two difficult problems for the post–New Testament community. The first arose from Christianity's Jewish background: How could God still be one and yet consist of both Father and Son, the Son sharing the Godness of God?[2] The second arose from the Hellenistic background of post–New Testament Christianity: How could one who shared the Godness of God (and who was therefore eternal, immutable, and impassible) become identified with a human being who was therefore temporal, mutable, and passible?

The Path to Chalcedon

During the three and a half centuries between the final redaction of the Fourth Gospel and the Chalcedonian definition, the church fathers wrestled with these problems, not just for speculation's sake, though there was a good deal of that, but also in order to defend the gospel against unbiblical perversions of it. These perversions contradicted the basic Christian experience. The two chief results of this long period of speculation, controversy, and conciliar definition were the Nicene Creed and the Chalcedonian formula of 325 and 451 C.E. respectively.

The relevant part of the Nicene Creed reads:

> We believe in one Lord, Jesus Christ
> the only Son of God,
> eternally begotten of the Father,
> God from God, Light from Light
> true God from true God,
> begotten not made,
> of one Being [*homoousios*] with the Father.
> Through him all things were made.
> For us and for our salvation
> he came down from heaven:
> by the power of the Holy Spirit
> he became incarnate from the Virgin Mary
> and was made man.[3]

This statement is concerned (over against Arianism) to assert the full deity of the Son. Both sides took preexistence for granted, but was the Son of like Being or of one Being with the Father? Nicaea could appeal particularly to the prologue of the Fourth Gospel, with its assertion that the preincarnate Logos was God, not just divine (*theos*, not *theios*), and its later assertion that the Incarnate One was the "only-begotten God" (John 1:18; see RSV margin).

Next the Chalcedonian formula turned its attention from the preexistent state of the Son of God to the historical life of Jesus and to the problem of how the same person could be both God and man. These are the salient phrases about the Incarnate One:

> at once complete in Godhead and complete in manhood
> truly God and truly man
> of one substance (*homoouios*) with the Father
>   as regards his Godhead
> of one substance with us as regards his manhood
> in two natures
> one person and subsistence.[4]

The Strengths and Weaknesses of Nicaea and Chalcedon

These venerable definitions have enjoyed undisputed authority in the East and in the West, among Catholics, Orthodox, and

Protestants alike until the time of the Enlightenment. They are doctrines that have certain strengths and advantages.

First, Chalcedon recognizes that there is only one Jesus of Nazareth and that this Jesus of Nazareth is one person. He is not like Strephon in Gilbert and Sullivan's *Iolanthe* (the son of a mortal father and a fairy mother, and therefore mortal from the waist down and immortal from the waist up). Jesus was not half a god and half a man. Nor was he a god who turned into a man, as in the Greek legends like the story of Philemon and Baucis. Nor may we accuse Chalcedon of indulging in speculation for its own sake. For all its unsatisfactory features, Leo's *Tome*, a kind of preparatory document for the council, shows that there was a real effort to speak about Jesus as he actually appeared in history.

Today, however, even among those theologians who would repudiate the charge of radicalism, there is an increasing awareness of the limitations and disadvantages of the Nicene-Chalcedonian christology. Despite the formal assertion that Jesus is one person, the council had great difficulty treating him as such. Again we see this from Leo's *Tome*,[5] where Christ seems to turn on his divinity or humanity according to the circumstances. When he is performing miracles, it is his divinity at work, when he is hungry or thirsty or tired—above all, when he is suffering—it is his humanity. Modern anthropology finds it difficult to conceive of a real historical being (as Chalcedon tried to insist that he was) acting in this way, and although Chalcedon cannot be faulted for it, the later Alexandrian or neo-Chalcedonian interpretation of the doctrine of the two natures argued for the impersonal character of Jesus' human nature. Only his divine nature was personal. This makes the core of Jesus' personality divine but not human. This interpretation is dangerously reminiscent of the earlier Apollinarian view that in Jesus the divine Logos replaced the human mind. Always these views, so prevalent at Alexandria and so influential at various times in the church at large, seem to want to carve out a hole from the humanity of Jesus and insert the divinity into that hole. The effect is always to make Jesus less than fully human. Chalcedon is often criticized as though the definition itself defined Christ's two natures in this way. But it did not: "anhypostasia" (impersonal humanity) is a later interpretation, not part of the original definition, and Chalcedon need not be interpreted in that way. Modern historical criticism and thinking, which has done so much to help us recover Jesus as a plausible figure in human history, makes it difficult for us today to go along with the kind of thinking that would make the humanity of Jesus impersonal. Whatever else he was, he was, as the biblical revelation testifies, a real human being. Chalcedon, properly interpreted, does not preclude us from recognizing that.

Closely related to the doctrine of an-hypostasia is the patristic church's conviction that God could neither be subject to change nor suffer—his immutability and impassibility which we touched on in Chapter 9. Of course, there is a biblical truth here, and it is not simply to be dismissed as a Greek idea. God is in a sense unchanging: unchanging in his *chesed w^{e}emeth*, his lovingkindness, his faithfulness, his steadfast covenant love. But even the Old Testament Yahweh is often said to "repent." God in his mercy and truth is flexible in reacting to the changing world of his creation. Only so could he be true to his *chesed*. The immutability of God must somehow be enlarged to include this flexibility. After all if, as Nicaea and Chalcedon affirmed, the Son of God, that aspect of his being in which he goes out of himself in revelatory and redemptive action, entered fully into the conditions of a human life, this must involve change in the being of God himself. Orthodoxy in a way acknowledged this when it spoke of the incarnation not as an act whereby God was changed into man but as an act in which "manhood was taken into God" (the Athanasian Creed). God is not quite what he was before that happened. And as for God's impassibility, that too, as we saw in Chapter 9, must be seriously qualified. It is the glory of God in the gospel that in the person of his Son he made himself completely and utterly vulnerable. This is the "weakness" of God about which Paul speaks (2 Cor. 13:4). Chalcedon, without directly intending it, made it difficult for Christian orthodoxy to recognize this weakness of God. The doctrine of the two natures assisted the development of the notion that Christ suffered in his human nature only and that his divine nature somehow remained immune. But should we blame Chalcedon for that? After all, there were those famous adverbs "without division, without separation." Maybe in some ways we need to take Chalcedon *more* seriously—at any rate at this point—than we have done in the past.

But perhaps the most serious problem with Chalcedon is that it has encouraged the wrong kind of christology from above. It has encouraged theology, ordinary church teaching, and popular piety to *start* with the deity of the Son of God and then to fit his humanity into the divinity. At all costs the divinity must remain inviolate, while the humanity is shortchanged. On the popular level, people argue, "Of course, Jesus could do miracles like changing water into wine. After all, he was God." Or again, people go to great lengths to defend Jesus from the kind of limited knowledge he displays in Mark 13:32. Jesus must have deliberately concealed what he really knew, by a process of accommodation. Again, Jesus' divinity has been used to support, for example, the Mosaic authorship of the Pentateuch, the Davidic origin of the psalms, or the historicity of the Jonah story. And as a result, the critical method has been repudiated in some quarters in order to defend the doctrine of the incarnation. All these are consequences of the wrong kind of christology from above, for such christologies begin with Jesus as God and proceed to examine his earthly history. In our christological thinking we must instead traverse ever and again the path taken by the church on its way to Nicaea and Chalcedon, namely, by starting with our experience of Jesus as a fully human phenomenon and from that humanity moving to affirm the definitive, eschatological presence of God. This in turn may lead us finally to confess our faith in the words of the historic definitions. But that faith is the conclusion, not the premise, of christology.

Dispensing with Preexistence and Incarnation

But do we need Nicaea and Chalcedon in order to confess our faith today? Its terminology (nature, person, and substance) is not ours. Can we not be content simply with confessing that we have found in the Christ event the definitive eschatological presence of God, a revelation and a salvation that can never be transcended, and leave it at that? This would in effect be to content ourselves with a theology of Jesus instead of having a christology proper.

A powerful and persuasive expression of this point of view has come from the pen of a German Lutheran New Testament scholar who has ventured into the field of systematics, Hans Grass.[6] He questions whether a preexistence-incarnation christology is really necessary. Grass bases his case on the fact that most of the New Testament authors got along all right without one, including the synoptic gospels, and Acts, the Catholic epistles apart from the Johannine, and Revelation. Moreover, those writings that do have such a christology—the Pauline corpus, the Johannine writings, and Hebrews—feature it only in traditional liturgical hymns and don't integrate it into the rest of their thinking. Accordingly, Grass would content himself with a "sending christology" of a salvation-historical kind. The only kind of preexistence he would admit is that of Jesus' predestination in the mind of God.

This is an attractive position. Unlike the older liberalism, which saw in Jesus a religious reformer, this proposal does recognize in Jesus the salvific, eschatological act of God. And Grass puts it forward with a real sense of the devotional loss of a condescendence christology, that "in Christ God descended to the lowest depths of our poor flesh and blood," so beautifully expressed in Luther's Christmas hymns. But this can remain as poetry. God did "come down" in Jesus, just as he "came down" in the Exodus (Exod. 3:8). The retention of the christological hymns simply as poetry would adequately integrate the experience of the Jesus phenomenon with the religious and moral experience of humanity in general and of Israel in particular. This would be to treat the wisdom imagery much in the same way that, according to James Dunn, pre-Christian Judaism did.

Grass is undoubtedly wrong when he includes the Johannine writings among those that fail to integrate the incarnational christology of their traditional hymns into their own christology. Rather, such integration is precisely the achievement of the Johannine school. Nor can this Johannine achievement be written off simply as a late development. John puts forward the claim that his theology is rooted in the Jesus tradition and is a legitimate development of it. In particular, his projection of the Father/Son christology, rooted as it is in Jesus' *Abba*-experience, claims to be an authentic development of Jesus' own self-understanding. If this claim is admitted, then we have to accept the fact that the Jesus phenomenon was a disclosure not simply of God in action but also of a dynamic process within the being of God himself. In Jesus' prayer life and concrete obedience we see God-in-himself and God-going-out-of-himself in their eternal, mutual relationship. To reject the Johannine development is to ignore a substantial part of the New Testament witness.[7] Consequently, if we are true to its entirety, we cannot rule out a preexistence-incarnation christology.

The Myth of God Incarnate

The publication in England of *The Myth of God Incarnate* by a group of British scholars was a *cause célèbre* for a year or two. These authors raised a number of objections to a christology of preexistence and incarnation, chief of which is that that doctrine is irretrievably mythological.[8] The most effective answer to the work is contained in James D. G. Dunn's *Christology in the Making*. Dunn has shown that the wisdom concept in pre-Christian Judaism (which, as is now generally agreed, is the source of preexistence-incarnation christology) is not really mythological.[9] Wisdom is not a divine being or hypostasis but a poetical personification of the activity of God. Dunn's careful exegesis of the New Testament christological hymns aside from John 1:1–18 has shown that the same is true there.[10] What Dunn did not go on to do was examine the way in which the Fourth Gospel integrated this hymnic christology with its development of the Father/Son christology of Jesus' *Abba*-experience. The christology of preexistence and incarnation is not mythological, but *an interpretation of Jesus' history in terms of a poetic tradition in the Old Testament and in Judaism*. We cannot therefore abandon the doctrine of the incarnational christology on the ground that it is pure mythology.

A Spirit Christology

A third attempt to eliminate the doctrine of the incarnation in the traditional sense of the word has come from the late Geoffrey Lampe. In his Bampton Lectures,[11] Lampe proposed to eliminate both the preexistence and the postexistence of Jesus. He would replace them with a christology of inspiration. God as Spirit means God as immanent and active in the world and in humanity. God as Spirit was active in the time B.C.E. in creating the world, in the history and experience of humanity in general, and especially in Israel's history. Further, God as Spirit was active in plenitude in the human person of Jesus of Nazareth. Next, God as Spirit continues to be active in the church and in the world as the "Spirit of Jesus." That is to say, everything God does henceforth toward the world and toward humanity he does *with reference to the Christ event*, making it present for salvation, for judgment, and for the enablement of human activity in accordance with his will. Jesus was merely the human bearer, but with a plenary inspiration of the Spirit. He did not share the very being of God as orthodoxy holds.

I found Lampe's proposal almost as attractive as the proposals of Grass—but not quite, because there is less emphasis in Lampe on the infinite distance between God and humanity and therefore between Jesus and humanity. Humanity's need, according to Lampe, seems to be more help along the same lines rather than radical redemption through a uniquely saving act of God. Also, Grass did make room for the postexistence of Jesus. The exalted life of Jesus seems quite basic to the New Testament and clearly presupposed or affirmed by all the New Testament writings, even by the Epistle of James. Grass was careful to eliminate only what seemed to him peripheral to the New Testament message. More specifically, Lampe seems to have misconstrued the role of the Spirit in the life of Jesus. The Spirit is not identical with the eschatological reality that is present in Jesus. Rather, the Spirit activates that reality. The ego of Jesus as the commissioned bearer of eschatological reality is prior to the enabling factor of the Holy Spirit. The Spirit calls forth, but is not identical with, that eschatological reality. This is attested by the "sending" formula, by the infancy narratives, and by the Johannine prologue, which states that the Word became flesh (John 1:14) prior to its activation by the Spirit at Jesus' baptism (John 1:33; 3:34). As Edwyn Hoskyns was always insisting, John's Gospel thus seeks to clarify the earlier tradition.

There have been many other interpretations of Jesus in recent years, all of them involving a rejection or at least a disregard of traditional orthodox christology. They include Jesus the revolutionary, Jesus the Zealot, Jesus the homosexual mystagogue, Jesus the magician.[12] These "modern" portraits are simply variants of the liberal Protestant Jesus so popular at the turn of the century.[13] George Tyrrell once accused Adolf von Harnack of looking down a well for the historical Jesus and seeing only the reflection of his own liberal Protestant face. The same is true, *mutatis mutandis*, of these latter-day reconstructions. And a recent attempt to revive the Christ myth theory (that Jesus was simply invented as a peg on which to hang the myth of a Savior God), hardly merits serious consideration.[14]

A Christological Proposal

Any viable christology today must, as we have insisted, start from below, from Jesus as a fully human person, a first-century Palestinian Jew with all his limitations. But in this fully human being faith discovers the presence, activity, and revelation of God himself. Even the neutral historian could in principle recognize that Jesus claimed to confront men and women with that eschatological presence and that his contemporaries either accepted it or rejected it. But he cannot *qua* historian accept or reject, prove or disprove, that claim.[15] Jesus' *Abba*-experience disclosed to further reflection an identity which was that of the eternal Son or Logos of God and offered a glimpse of the inner Being of God. Within that Being are two (or three, if we count later reflections on the Spirit) aspects. We call them "aspects" as a neutral if not entirely adequate designation for what later christology called "persons" in a highly technical sense. There is an aspect of the Being of God which is God-in-himself, the ground of Being, and there is an aspect which is God-going-out-of-himself in self-communicating love. (And, to include the Holy Spirit, there is a God-creating-in-believers-the-response-to-his-self-communication). Finally, the divinity of Jesus is not an insertion into or a substitute for some part of his humanity, nor is part of him human and part divine. In his full humanity he is the definitive presence of God in-the-act-of-self-communication, *Deus pro nobis*, of the same God who was for us in creation, preservation, general revelation, and Israel's special revelation. There is no part of his humanity that is not such a revelation. This is the truth we find in Nicaea and Chalcedon. But we cannot simply repeat their language today, adequate as it no doubt was in its own day and age.

Summary

As christology developed in the New Testament period, there was a shift of focus from the end of Jesus' way to its beginning. The "sending" christology and the identification of Jesus as the incarnation of preexistent wisdom shifted the focus from the end to the beginning of Jesus' way, to the moment of his entry into the world, and to what preceded it. Johannine reflection further led to the projection of the Father/Son relationship to this preexistent phase. This led to a further shift from salvation history to ontology. These developments created problems for the post–New Testament church. How could the Father be God and the Son be God and God be one? How could Jesus be both human and divine? The definitive answer to these questions was set forth by way of confessional affirmation (rather than theological explanation) in the Nicene creed and Chalcedonian formula: the former defining the Son as of one Being with the Father (*homoousios*), the latter defining Jesus' divine humanity as one of two natures in one person.

The positive and negative features of these definitions were explored, and modern objections and alternatives were investigated. Nicaea preserved the community's experience of Jesus as a recognition of the God who had already been at work. Chalcedon preserved the twofold nature of the Christian experience of Jesus: the fully human person in which God's definitive revelation and redemption were embodied. The modern attempts to replace christology by a theology of Jesus or a pneumatology appeared attractive, but were inadequate to the primary experience of the Jesus phenomenon and to subsequent reflection upon it. Today we must have a christology that starts from below and that finds the divinity *in* the whole humanity of Jesus.

FOR FURTHER READING

Hanson, A. T. *Grace and Truth: A Study in the Incarnation.* London: SPCK, 1975. A noted Anglo-Irish scholar defends the preexistence-incarnation christology of the Johannine prologue as necessary for Christian faith today.

Hanson, R. P. C. *The Attractiveness of God: Essays in Christian Doctrine.* London: SPCK, 1973. Like his brother, A. T. Hanson (see previous entry), R. P. C. Hanson defends the christology of Nicaea but is critical of the two-natures dogma of Chalcedon on the ground that it tends to do less than justice to the full humanity of Jesus. See chap. 5, "The Chalcedonian Formula: A Declaration of Good Intentions," pp. 96–115.

Pannenberg, W. *Jesus—God and Man.* Eng. trans. L. and D. Priebe. Philadelphia: Westminster Press; London: SCM Press, 1968. The best history of christology from the New Testament to the present day with critical and constructive observations for contemporary christological statement.

Wiles, M. *The Making of Christian Doctrine.* New York and Cambridge: Cambridge University Press, 1967. A study of the principles of doctrinal development (including christology) in the patristic era.

————. *Explorations in Theology 4.* London: SCM Press, 1979. Nine essays by a radical theologian, including "Christology in an Age of Historical Studies," pp. 28–40.

Robinson, J. A. T. *The Human Face of God.* Philadelphia: Westminster Press, 1973. Based on the Hulsean Lectures for 1970, this work is primarily a systematic attempt to criticize and to restate in terms of process philosophy the orthodox doctrine of the incarnation.

Hick, J., ed. *The Myth of God Incarnate.* Philadelphia: Westminster Press, 1977. A collection of essays written mainly by members of the theological faculty of the University of Birmingham, England. It is the preeminent christological statement of the radical theology of the 1970s, with its abandonment of preexistence-incarnation christology in favor of a "historical" christology.

For the subsequent debate see:

Green, E. W., ed. *The Truth of God Incarnate.* Grand Rapids: Wm. B. Eerdmans, 1977. A hastily compiled reply to Hick's *The Myth of God Incarnate* by some more conservative scholars.

Goulder, M., ed. *Incarnation and Myth: The Debate Continued.* Grand Rapids: Wm. B. Eerdmans, 1979. Essays in criticism and defense of the *Myth of God Incarnate.*

Macquarrie, J. "Tradition, Truth, and Christology." *HeyJ* 21 (1980): 365–75. A brief discussion of the relationship between tradition and truth in formulating christology which seeks to mediate between a static view of tradition and one that would cut the truth of christology loose from its mediation by tradition that claims to have originated in a specific act of God.

NOTES

1. This element of "recognition" expressed in the preexistence christology is well brought out in A. T. Hanson, *Grace and Truth: A Study in the Incarnation* (London: SPCK, 1975), pp. 64–95, in connection with the Johannine prologue. In itself, however, such a recognition would require only a "theology of Jesus"—the God already known was present in Jesus—not a doctrine of personal preexistence. Only the Johannine Father/Son christology requires that.

2. John 1:1, *theos ēn ho logos*, not *theios ēn ho logos*. The anarthrous *theos* is untranslatable. It means "shared the God-ness of God" but without being inexhaustibly what God was. The New English Bible's "what God was, the Word was" is misleading if that is taken to mean "*all* that God was, the Word was."

3. Translation from *Prayers We Have in Common*, prepared by the International Consultation on English Texts, 2d rev. ed. (Philadelphia: Fortress Press, 1975).

4. Translation from *The Book of Common Prayer*, 1979.

5. For an English translation of Leo's *Tome*, see *Documents of the Christian Church*, ed. H. Bettenson (New York and London: Oxford University Press, 1944), pp. 69–72.

6. H. Grass, *Christliche Glaubenslehre* (Stuttgart: Kohlhammer, 1975), 1:79–108. Hans Grass is the brother of Günter Grass.

7. My teacher, Sir Edwyn Hoskyns, was always profoundly convinced that Johannine theology is not mythological and speculative but rooted in the synoptic and synopticlike tradition. This is already expressed in his earliest published essay, "Gen. i-iii and St. John's Gospel," *JTS* 21 (1920): 210–18, and later in his two posthumously published works edited by N. Davey, *The Fourth Gospel* (London: Faber & Faber, 1947²), and *Crucifixion-Resurrection* (London: SPCK, 1981). But Hoskyns's recognition of development was inadequate.

8. *The Myth of God Incarnate*, ed. J. Hick (Philadelphia: Westminster Press, 1977), esp. M. Goulder's essay, "The Two Roots of the Christian Myth," pp. 64–86. Goulder finds the source of preexistence-incarnation christology in a hypothetical Samaritan myth. This is open to the same objections as the Bultmannian Gnostic redeemer myth. See J. D. G. Dunn, *Christology in the Making: A New Testament Inquiry into the Origins of the Doctrine of the Incarnation* (Philadelphia: Westminster Press, 1980), p. 277, n. 67, and the literature given there.

9. Dunn, *Christology in the Making*, pp. 168–76.

10. Ibid., pp. 176–96, 206–12, 239–47.

11. G. W. H. Lampe, *God as Spirit* (Oxford: At the Clarendon Press, 1977).

12. For Jesus as revolutionary, see J. Carmichael, *The Death of Jesus* (New York: Macmillan Co., 1963); for Jesus as Zealot, see S. G. F. Brandon, *Jesus and the Zealots* (Manchester, Eng.: Manchester University Press, 1967); for Jesus as homosexual mystagogue, see M. Smith, *The Secret Gospel* (New York: Harper & Row, 1973), and for Jesus as magician, see idem, *Jesus the Magician* (New York: Harper & Row, 1978).

13. See the warning by H. J. Cadbury, *The Peril of Modernizing Jesus* (New York: Macmillan Co., 1937), a book all too neglected by those who perpetrate lives of Jesus.

14. G. A. Wells, *The Jesus of the Early Christians: A Study in Christian Origins* (London: Pemberton Books, 1971).

15. At the conclusion of their historical investigation of Jesus, E. C. Hoskyns and N. Davey wrote: "Here, then, the historian is driven to lay down his pen, not because he is defeated; not because his material has proven incapable of historical treatment; but because he is forced to judge—to believe or disbelieve" (*The Riddle of the New Testament* [London: Faber & Faber, 1931], p. 182).

11

Christology and Culture

Looking at the Twentieth Century

The New Testament writers appropriated language and symbols from their culture to express, understand, and interpret Jesus. Diversity and constant creativity is typical of the relationship between biblical traditions and the surrounding cultures. It has been described as a "sacred discontent." The Bible is unwilling to formulate an unchanging, stable mythology as the basis for an enduring political or social order. Instead, one finds the Bible constantly challenging the presuppositions on which humans try to construct their own order. It insists that order can be founded only on what God has established. Consequently, the Bible runs through myths and symbols at an alarming rate. Western society, built on that biblical tradition, shows the same orientation. No other society is so preoccupied with unmasking, undercutting, even "demythologizing," the traditions that would appear to form its foundation. One observer comments, "The Western world uses up myth at a tremendous rate, and often has to borrow frantically from other cultures, or to allow the oscillations that time and chance will bring but which mythological societies will dampen effectively."[1] Though not a comforting prospect, this observation enables us to gain perspective on the discontent frequently voiced over our twentieth-century loss of faith or of a common set of values. The media may make us more aware of such patterns of change, but the dynamic that drives us to constant questioning and reformulation is not the sudden creation of technology, it has been part of our cultural heritage from the beginning. Before we lament our "alienation," we should take stock of its positive contributions to the development of our culture.[2]

As more people become aware of changes in our culture, there is more pressure on religious institutions to resist, to provide fixed patterns of faith, doctrine, and worship. Yet such a demand fails to recognize the internal dynamic of the biblical heritage on which those institutions are built. Faith never provided a hold on an "unchanging" reality. It demanded faithfulness, trust in God's Word and promise for a future that was often obscured by the turmoil in which God's people lived. We have seen that both Mark and John formulated a vision of Jesus for communities in turmoil. They both began with the fundamental image of the cross, not some unchanging beatitude, as the basic sign of God's salvation. That symbol enabled them to make contact with the suffering and confusion in their own situations. Unless christology can make sense of the experiences of believing Christians in a concrete situation, it remains the preserve of a theologically trained elite, a museum piece from our past.

Christology faces the challenge of showing that the message that salvation comes into the world through Jesus can make sense out of twentieth-century experience. Christians must overcome their suspicion of science, technology, and other elements of modern culture so that they can take seriously the new pictures of the universe and humanity that are emerging in our time. Serious dialogue does not mean accepting all elements of the new image of the world without question or modification, just as the New Testament did not appropriate older symbols without modification. Failure to dialogue will deprive religion of any voice in the pressing public issues of our time. Failure to form an adequate image of the scientific, social, and political realities of the modern world forces religion into the sphere of private experience. Biblical faith has never required protection from the world.[3]

Our needs for salvation in the twentieth century are not the same as those in the first century. The memory of Jesus must address people's questions about salvation. Jesus cannot simply be a political revolutionary or a source of psychological enlightenment according to the latest personal or regional fad.[4] The public side of the death of Jesus engages his followers in a struggle with the structures of evil and violence. Part of the biblical memory is a refusal to forget the sufferings of the past as "ended" and unimportant. No future can be built which depends on the oppression of people. The necessity to transform all suffering implied in the cross raises serious questions for all projects of liberation which think that the Messiah (*Christos*) is to be identified with the victorious and not with the suffering.[5]

An Evolving Humanity and the Christological Affirmation

Many people would point out that humanity is still evolving through the cultural forms with which it has clothed itself. They see in the Christ a symbol for the goal of that process. One example of such evolutionism is to be found in transcendental christologies, which see in Jesus the fulfillment of all that we now know the human person to be in relation to the transcendent source of everything, God, as well as in relation to others and to the self.[6] Continuity with the past is maintained because of the transcendental unity of the concept "person." Such christologies often appear unsatisfactory because the concerns of Jesus of Nazareth in the first century (as well as anything that could reasonably have been meant by "Self" in that context) belong to a culture so different from ours that we do not seem to be the same people. Our consciousness would appear to have been radically changed by the vast changes of the technological and media revolution.

Edward Schillebeeckx has wrestled with this problem more deeply than most theologians, because he insists that the historical Jesus and his aims must remain at the foundation of christology. Christians recognize that the language in which they express their faith reflects particular understandings of the human world. At the same time, we must acknowledge that cultural change takes place on different levels. Facts and information change rapidly. Changes in the fundamental model by which a society defines itself and reality are much slower. At a deeper level still, one finds that the structures of human consciousness, which seem to have developed along with the human species, are slow to change.[7] These basic structures of consciousness make human models of the world possible. The various levels of consciousness and change explain why images of reality that have lost touch with the world of facts and information may continue to function well enough for those who use them. An outdated model cannot perform one important function, however. It cannot point to the future. Those who claim or act as if the Jesus of history exercises no critical function over against our christology rely on a model of historical evolution which decides that since our judgments about the past are only probable, no person or event can have absolute value. It neglects the "humanizing importance" of the human ability to recall the past. That past teaches the Christian that the God of Jesus insists on identification with the persecuted. Further, the universality implied by the universality of God's rule can be mediated to the world only through a particular community, the church.[8]

Another evolutionary approach to the christological problem presents the incarnation as an event in the evolution of human consciousness. Christ is said to represent or express the archetype of the "Self." Other representations of this archetype are also possible. The Self represents an inner salvation which each individual must work out for himself or herself in overcoming the hidden dynamics and dualism that come about with the formation of the human ego.[9] In earlier times, people could project psychological realities onto stories and leaders. They reached psychological integration through the mediation of ritual and story. But projection of psychic dynamics "out there" no longer works for the twentieth-century Westerner. Consciousness has become the norm. Therefore, religious symbols are effective only when they are worked through by each individual in the process of transformation. Christianity must touch base with this project of psychological transformation if its theological language is to remain effective.

A more moderate position than that dependent on Jungian analysis has been proposed by Sebastian Moore. He does not propose a reduction of the reality of Jesus to the psychic Christ symbol, but he suggests that we begin to view Jesus as the exemplary one who evokes the real self of the human. The human psyche needs such an evocative exemplar because it exists in a state of generic guilt, of estrangement from God—the mysterious "other" in reality with which all humans are in some way involved. The dynamics that generate such guilt are based in the various strategies by which humans close themselves off from that "other."

Guilt in the face of our failure to acknowledge the other will be healed only when it becomes clear that God is love and not power. This manifestation of the priority of love over power, evidenced in the cross, requires that God testify to the divinity of Jesus, just as the Fourth Gospel insists God does. His divinity does not mean that Jesus is a universal human archetype equivalent to the cultural symbols humanity has brought forth from its collective unconscious. Many of the christological titles—Lord, King, Messiah, Son of Man—have archetypal dimensions. They represent cultural symbols used to mediate the reality of Jesus' divinity, but they should not be confused with that divinity as though it were somehow tied to those symbols. Each culture must draw on its own symbolic resources to express the truth about Jesus. At the same time, it is necessary to remember that the universal self evoked by Jesus lies beyond human conceptualization, since it is not bound by the dynamics of generic guilt and power that typify the human psyche.[10]

Similar questions about the relationship of the gospel to psychodynamics have been raised by Donald Gelpi. He argues that the interaction of pleasure and aggression fundamental to the formation of the human ego in psychological theory can never give rise to the symbolics of atoning love found in Jesus.[11] Therefore, he concludes that the new reality of atoning love presented in Jesus must have been realized in an individual. As such it is a surprise to any theory of human ego-formation.[12] But individuals are not brought into that psychic transformation simply by contact with its symbolization in the gospel. They must belong to the "Spirit-filled" community, which is the locus for appropriating the new, saving image of Christ as Self.

These reflections on the significance of Jesus for human self-hood represent a sustained attempt to grapple with the question about Jesus in twentieth-century terms. This concern does not absolutize our perspective, but it recognizes that our culture sets the conditions within which we either find salvation or we do not.[13] Clearly, the process cannot be one-sided. The theologian does not go to the academic marketplace and buy a psychological or social theory, plug in the gospel, and cry, "Eureka! Cultural relevance!" Many theologians see the danger of a psychological or

symbolic approach to christology as nominalism, that is, a christological view which holds that Jesus is called Savior but that the
real work of salvation takes place only as individuals are transformed through their appropriation of the Christ symbol. As long
as the psyche of an individual is transformed, the relationship between the particular Christ image and either the gospel story or
the historical person of Jesus doesn't matter. Theologians caution
that christology must have a "realist" dimension. What happened
in Jesus has changed humanity's position over against the "mysterious other," whether or not that change is appropriated by individuals or cultures.[14] Theologians who use psychological models
to speak about the reality of Jesus make it clear that those models
must be brought into dialogue with theological reflection on the
human person.

Toward a Viable Image of the People of God

Christologies based on psychological models are often criticized
for their starting point, a fascination with the individual self.
Some theologians respond by modeling the self in its relational
openness toward, and even formation by, others,[15] or they insist
that the community of believers is necessary for the saving transformation of the individual.[16] The starting point itself may be
problematic, however. Community as a collection of such selves,
even in relation to one another, may not be an adequate image for
the world in which Christians find themselves. Problems that we
fail to master adequately in our imagination have a way of explod-
ing on us when we have to confront them on the practical level.[17]
Viable and appropriate images of human community are becoming increasingly problematic. Johannes Metz argues that the most
pressing political questions of our time are really questions about
salvation. They concern who is entitled to use what resources and
how they are to be used, for example.[18] Yet approaches to these
problems which begin with preoccupations about the individual
self as owner of private property and entitled to a certain form of
life maintained by that economic arrangement do not provide
fruitful ways of imaging the problems we face on a global scale.

Once again, theologians must be careful to recognize the contours and limitations of the imagination in particular cultures. We have lost much of our rootedness in history and nature. Our artists often portray the human person as Protean, as a slippery creation of personal or social projection with emptiness at its core. Furthermore, our literal-minded approach to mythic and symbolic language has a negative, even frightening, side. Those who cannot appreciate the revealing power of symbols seem destined to enact ever more uncontrolled expressions of human imagination. We even appear willing to accept broken, violent, and uncontrolled ecstasies.[19] Christians may have to dig back into the fuller imagination of the world that belongs to their tradition.[20] There are abroad dangerous myths that can be countered only by a better myth. Some of these dangerous visions are all too familiar: the empty self; the call to create and even recreate oneself; the violence of and even hunger for revolt, wiping the slate clean, as a solution to the complexities of the world; the myth of the innocence of those who seek to overthrow unjust systems; a fear of authority which can see authority only in demonic terms; and even the supposition that the powers of salvation are located within the human self, just waiting to be brought out by proper manipulation of consciousness. All these visions mask an anarchy that would destroy human order. They cannot be allowed to co-opt the biblical vision of the people of God. The biblical vision requires images that provide theological ordering on the cosmic scale.[21] One of the most important elements in that vision is the confrontation with evil. Christianity does not seek a mystic transcendence that reduces evil to the illusion of a self caught in the material world. The self-discipline and purgation which Christian spirituality associates with overcoming evil belongs to the biblical commitment to wrestle with evil in the public sphere, not merely in private. The cross makes it clear that the victory over evil costs the victor. Christians experience the victory over evil as decisively won yet incomplete. Such a victory requires that disorder be resolved at a level deeper than that which might be expected if the conquest were a matter of imposing superior power, whether human or divine. The covenant spirituality of the biblical traditions addresses humans in their many-sided dealings with creation, history, society, and politics. It rejects fascination with the

Spirit or with "raised consciousness" for its own sake. Jesus did not found a sect devoted to cultivating its own private experience of God and salvation. Jesus insisted on renewing the Old Testament images of the rule of God over the creation.[22]

The Christian can apply the fundamental structure of the biblical vision as a discernment of spirits over against the visions of humanity presented by our culture. Biblical salvation was never a mirror of its culture, nor was it limited to some partial segment of reality, even one so dear to us as the self. It has always required us to wrestle with the anarchy that threatens human order. Amos Wilder has suggested criteria of adequacy that Christians should apply to the visions of salvation with which they are confronted:

1. What is the quality and scope of the inner life presented? Does it take into account the many-sided relationships of the human person?
2. What are the human and moral ramifications of a particular vision? Does it, for example, create an "innocence" that can be engaged in violence?
3. What is the outreach of a particular vision? How are conflicts resolved?
4. What is the relationship between ecstatic experiences and the actualities of life both before and after such experiences?

Ecstasy, for example, in the New Testament has a critical orientation, as in Revelation, where it emerges from the experience of tribulation. Paul insists that the suffering and not the spiritual power of the apostle legitimates his ministry. Thus, ecstasy in the New Testament emerges in the process of clarifying the experience of wrestling with the world. There is no shortcut to vision, to poetry, or to wisdom.[23]

Our christological images must fit the cosmological scope of the biblical vision. The cross reveals the meaning of divine messianism. It contradicts any claim that salvation is delivered through power. God does not promote his cause over against creation through violence. Instead, he comes to that creation through identification, "taking the *morphē* of a servant," as the Philippians hymn puts it (Phil. 2:6–11). The lordship of Christ remains hidden and incomplete until all is handed over to the Father. These qualities of weakness, hiddenness, and incompleteness imply that the divine continues its involvement with humanity and creation. The New Testament sees the new community that acknowledges Jesus' lordship and its experiences of salvation as the key to understanding the truth of Jesus. Through them, God's salvation is mediated to humanity at large.[24]

Christology addresses different audiences. Members of that community of faith already have at least an unformed, unconditional "yes" to Jesus as salvation. For them, the question is "How can we think of Jesus as God or of God as Jesuslike?" Those who are outside that community ask a slightly different christological question: "How can a particular human, Jesus, be God or be the source of salvation for the cosmos?"[25] The Johannine struggle with christological affirmations has shown us how the debate with nonbelievers pushed the church into deeper reflection on the implications of its christological insights. All the christologies in the New Testament begin with the conviction that in some way Jesus does what only God does. This claim becomes clearly articulated in the Johannine tradition. It also forces Christians to engage in something of a war of images. None of the traditional messianic images could adequately express the combination of God's salvation and human person found in Jesus.[26] Our questions about christology and the modern images of salvation face a similar dilemma, though we may approach that dilemma from the other side. We want to know how salvation comes to us from God. Or, better, how can human mediation of liberation or salvation escape the traps of violence, partial realization, and creation of new forms of slavery that seem to corrupt human efforts? In short, how do humans act for God and for themselves?

Summary

The first level at which the question of christology and culture is posed represents the vast cultural differences between the first century C.E. and our own day. The symbols and images of that time might have nothing to say to people today. Indeed, had the biblical tradition been the mythological base for a cultural system, its symbols would have perished with that system. A more penetrating look at the relationship between the biblical traditions and culture shows that their dynamic of discontent, even of demythologizing, represents the roots of Western culture. We even orchestrate experiences of "loss of faith" into the life cycle of our children. Faithfulness in the Bible does not guarantee a stable world. It points to the purposes of God in a flux of events that seems destined never to leave the people comfortable in the land—or in their religious and social imagery. Christians are challenged on this level to abandon the myth of a stable past and tradition, to overcome their suspicion of the world as a godless and irreligious place, and to get on with the task of addressing the questions of salvation that emerge in the realities of the twentieth century.

The biblical foundations of our culture are not the only guarantee we have that the biblical traditions can be so employed. We may also argue that the evolving human self is not so far divorced from its origins as the rapid changes on the level of fact and technology might lead us to believe. Contemporary concerns with the varied dimensions of human selfhood provide another starting point for christology. Some focus on the Christ symbol as a universal archetype of the human "Self." The power of the symbol lies in its ability to bring together those opposites whose reconciliation is crucial to the transition from ego-center to self-center. The believer must discover the power of that symbol in the transformation of his or her consciousness. A more realist christology questions the reduction of Jesus to symbol. This approach finds the Christ as an image of atoning love which runs counter to the archetypes that are spontaneously generated by the human psyche. Psychoanalytic theory can only imagine such a love as a negation of the reality principle, an archaic projection of infantile desire. Consequently, the incarnation of the divine and the suffering and death of Jesus as the way to salvation contain a "surprise" for the human ego. Had such a self not happened, humanity would not have invented it. The reality of that happening is also quite independent of its subjective appropriation by humans. That reality is the focus of divine grace.

Psychological imagery itself is too bound up with the development of Western consciousness to provide an adequate, cosmic vision of salvation for the world that is now emerging across the globe. At yet a deeper level, the encounter between christology and culture involves a war of images. The peoples of the globe are torn by restricted images of salvation, by a fateful complicity of innocence and violence, and by an inability to formulate images that include individuals, nature, and society in a whole. A fear of authority, verging on paranoia, makes the human the creator of self and salvation. Evil lies "out there" in the system, in business, in science, in technology, in government, in the military-industrial complex, and so on. Liberate the human from bondage to that litany of powers, and an innocent new human will emerge. Often this emergence is said to be signaled by the ecstasies of consciousness-raising. People experience their own innocence and freedom in the transcendence granted by revolutionary consciousness. The biblical tradition responds with a firm "no" to all such claims. God does not save creation in the ecstasy of a messianic revolution or in the transcendence experienced in a new consciousness. Instead, the Messiah suffers. The Messiah identifies with the most helpless and despised—not even the heroes of a revolution. The Messiah conquers the powers and death and yet leaves them in place. Indeed, the ending of the messianic story still seems to reside in human hands, those of a new people of God to be sure, but people nonetheless, spirit-filled, to be sure, but not yet transformed into the image of Christ. Confessing that there is no other name by which salvation comes to humanity commits the Christian to a project of faithfulness amid all the confusion and turmoil of God's creation.

FOR FURTHER READING

Gilkey, L. *Society and the Sacred: Toward a Theology of Culture in Decline*. New York: Crossroad, 1981. Gilkey's work provides an excellent comprehensive introduction to the problem of theology and culture. He discusses the problems created by the confrontation with modernity in the sociopolitical realm and the scientific realm. He suggests that cultural and religious pluralism requires a rethinking of the relationship between Christ and the saving activity of God. Christ may manifest God's saving activity without being the cause or the sole embodiment of it.

Driver, T. *Christ in a Changing World: Toward an Ethical Christology*. New York: Crossroad, 1981. Driver argues that the modern situation of change and development demands that theologians abandon all static categories, whether "biblicism" or "Christ once and for all" foundations of theology. The significance of the resurrection, he suggests, is that both God and Christ change along with the human world. Anything less would turn living faith into blind support for an ideology that seeks to arrest or repress the inevitable development of humanity.

Schillebeeckx, E. *Jesus: An Experiment in Christology*. Eng. trans. H. Hoskins. New York: Seabury Press, 1979. Schillebeeckx agrees that the pressing questions of salvation in each age must shape its christology, but he questions the simplistic models of cultural change which suppose that all levels of the human life-world change at the same rate or to the same degree that the technological world changes. He argues that the historical Jesus and his purposes must remain the foundation of any christology.

Tracy, D. *The Analogical Imagination: Christian Theology and the Culture of Pluralism*. New York: Crossroad, 1981. Tracy seeks to use the "hermeneutic of the classic" to elucidate the problem of continuity and change within the tradition. The New Testament witnesses to Jesus as paradigmatic event which both discloses and conceals—as any symbolic discourse does—who God is and who we are. The trust that life patterned on that of Jesus can become the *ethos* for human life must also be mediated through a believing community. Consequently, the christological task should not be conceived as "historical Jesus," on one side, over against a monolithic "modern culture," on the other side. The confluence of a variety of mediating structures, and different "publics," must be part of any theological discourse.

Schneidau, H. *Sacred Discontent: The Bible and Western Tradition*. Berkeley and Los Angeles: University of California Press, 1977. Schneidau argues that there is a fundamental dynamic of "discontent" and unmasking of cultural pretensions in the biblical material. This drive stands at the root of the Western cultural tradition, including our present concerns with change and demythologizing.

Wilder, A. *Theopoetic: Theology and the Religious Imagination*. Philadelphia: Fortress Press, 1976. Wilder discusses the symbolics of Christian vision in relation to literature and the arts. Not all contemporary symbolics are adequate to the biblical vision.

Homans, P. *Jung in Context: Modernity and the Making of a Psychology*. Chicago: University of Chicago Press, 1979. Homans describes the development of Jungian theory as a claim to provide a "religious alternative" for people in the twentieth century.

Moore, S. *The Fire and the Rose Are One*. New York: Seabury Press, 1980. Moore's meditative and poetic style of theological reflection embodies an attempt to bring together theological insights and psychological conceptions of the human psyche. Neither side can remain unchanged by the encounter. Moore continues to maintain a realist

christology. Christ represents a real breakthrough in the psychodynamics of human guilt in face of the divine.

NOTES

1. See H. Schneidau, *Sacred Discontent: The Bible and Western Tradition* (Berkeley and Los Angeles: University of California Press, 1977),
p. 14.

2. See ibid., pp. 1–49. Schneidau suggests that we even build "loss of
faith" into the life cycle with tales like the Easter Bunny, the Tooth
Fairy, and Santa Claus (pp. 48–49).

3. See H. Küng, *Does God Exist?* (New York: Doubleday & Co., 1980)
ךp 87–140.

4. E. Schillebeeckx, *Jesus: An Experiment in Christology*, Eng. trans.
H. Hoskins (New York: Seabury Press, 1979), pp. 60–70.

5. J. Metz, *Faith in History and Society* (New York: Seabury Press,
1980). pp. 100–35; J. Moltmann, *The Crucified God* (New York: Harper
& Row, 1974), pp. 317–41.

6. W. Thompson, *Jesus, Lord and Savior: A Theopathic Christology and
Soteriology* (New York: Paulist Press, 1980), pp. 162–92.

7. See F. Sulloway, *Freud, Biologist of the Mind* (New York: Basic
Books, 1979), pp. 3–5, 365–92.

8. Schillebeeckx, *Jesus*, pp. 577–94.

9. See the discussion of Jung's psychology as "religion" for
twentieth-century humans in P. Homans, *Jung in Context: Modernity and
the Making of a Psychology* (Chicago: University of Chicago Press, 1979),
pp. 161–209.

10. See S. Moore, *The Fire and the Rose Are One* (New York: Seabury
Press, 1980), pp. 129–31.

11. See Paul Ricoeur's critique of the infantile and the archaic in the
Freudian understanding of love in *Freud and Philosophy* (New Haven,
Conn.: Yale University Press, 1970), pp. 548–51.

12. D. Gelpi, *Experiencing God* (New York: Paulist Press, 1978), pp.
187–89.

13. Schillebeeckx, *Jesus*, pp. 586–89.

14. But see the defense of nominalist processive christology by G.
Rupp, *Christologies and Cultures* (The Hague: Mouton, 1974), pp. 38–47.
Rupp argues that atonement must be viewed as a process which tran-
spires over history and which is known only in the results of Christ's
work in believers and communities that appropriate its benefits. Such a
process is sponsored by the images of the biblical narrative (p. 167).

15. So Thompson, *Jesus, Lord and Savior.*

16. So Gelpi, *Experiencing God.*

17. The necessity for adequate theological imagination is similar to the

necessity for the thought experiment in modern physics. Such experiments are not predictions. They are models of developments "with which we shall have to come to terms theoretically before we can handle them practically"; see F. Dyson, *Disturbing the Universe* (New York: Harper & Row, 1979), p. 197.

18. J. Metz, *The Emergent Church* (New York: Crossroad, 1981), pp. 48–81.

19. See A. Wilder, *Theopoetic: Theology and the Religious Imagination* (Philadelphia: Fortress Press, 1976), pp. 34–40.

20. In ibid. (p. 17) Wilder suggests that some of the contemporary fascination with the "mysticism" of non-Christian traditions represents an unwillingness to grapple with the issues represented by the biblical vision of reality.

21. Ibid., p. 4.

22. Ibid., pp. 11–22.

23. Ibid., 71–72.

24. The turn toward the New Testament experience of salvation in the second volume of Schillebeeckx' christology reflects this side of the New Testament tradition. See E. Schillebeeckx, *Christ: The Experience of Jesus as Lord* (New York: Seabury Press, 1980), pp. 31–64.

25. Moore, *The Fire and the Rose Are One*, p. 157.

26. Ibid., pp. 152–57.

12

The Ultimacy of Christ in a Pluralistic World

The Problem of Religious Pluralism

Christianity emerged as a combination of universalism and exclusivism. The messianic salvation made possible through Jesus was to be addressed to all humanity, not just to the Jews. On the other hand, Jesus was acknowledged as the final revelation of God. There could be no other. We have seen that while the Johannine tradition developed universal symbols for Jesus, it also insisted that no other religious traditions had validity. The Son is the only revelation of the Father. That revelation is the norm for evaluating all religious symbols.

Twentieth-century Christians, faced with the religious pluralism of the globe in each day's news, are often uneasy with this exclusive universalism. The application of the Old Testament condemnation of idolatry to the great religious traditions of humanity no longer seems viable. Both scholarship and the adoption of those traditions by others in our society are making their religious insights known to people. The old "lost in darkness and corruption" language about non-Christian religions seems to be a dangerous misrepresentation that could leave us unable to deal socially and politically, not to mention religiously, with most of the world. Many Christian theologians are asking what the study of those traditions might contribute to Christian theology. The major church bodies have reminded their members that the truth inherent in other religions is to be respected. The Christian then wonders how, if at all, the insistence on the uniqueness or ultimacy of Christ could be maintained in such a world. What of the claim that Christ is mediator of salvation, if we must also recognize that there is saving mediation between God and humanity in other traditions as well?

A Unifying Drive Behind the Diversity of Religions?

The primary assumption from the Christian side—and not necessarily from other traditions—must be that the God encountered by other traditions is the same God Christians encounter in Jesus. If we also hold that Jesus is God, not merely another human religious leader, then we must acknowledge that humanity's religious traditions will not go beyond what has been revealed in Jesus. That need not require us to deny that salvation and communion with God can be found in another religious tradition, any more than we would deny the saving value of faith for the people of God in the Old Testament.[1] In fact, it is almost impossible to raise the question of the relationship between Christianity and other religious traditions in the ways in which it may be raised with regard to Judaism. A real dialogue between Christianity and those religious "forerunners" must still take place on the same level of seriousness as that between Christianity and Judaism—or that between Christianity and its Greek heritage. Paul Ricoeur suggests that until we have such a common tradition with other non-Western peoples of the world, dialogue with them remains an intellectual exercise. Their traditions cannot illuminate who we are in the same way that our classical and biblical traditions do.[2]

The retreat into personalism leads some Christians to focus the question of ultimacy on the humanity and divinity of Christ, as if a properly formulated anthropology could prove the uniqueness of Jesus. We would remain closer to the biblical perspective if we approached the question of the ultimacy of salvation in Christ from the perspective of God's faithfulness to the covenant. That faithfulness extends beyond the office of Messiah (*Christos*), which is defined in a specific situation of the people of God. It is a contingent fact dependent on the history of sinfulness of that people and also on the existence of the remnant of faithful ones within Israel. Once we recognize the contingency and limitation of the messianic office, we can see that God remains free to communicate the same faithfulness in other ways. Such ways may be embodied in other religious traditions. Further, the same principle holds for "space theology," for life forms elsewhere in the universe. They need not experience salvation through the crucified and risen Jesus in order to experience God's faithfulness to creation.[3]

Jesus' revelation of God nonetheless stresses one facet of God's faithfulness to creation so clearly that we might expect it to be represented in other revelations: God's commitment to the weak, to the suffering, and even to the evil side of that creation. Can we say that we encounter "the same" God if we do not find the same refusal to act out of the pretensions of power, of innocence, of "divinity" that is so prominent a feature of the imaging of God in Jesus? Such a question can hardly be answered by an outsider to those other traditions, since an outsider can hardly appreciate the shape that faith and the issues of salvation take in the same way the believer does.[4]

Even as we take the unity of God as the starting point for a Christian vision of the wider religious scene, we must still ask about the dynamics of the new order of humanity that seems to be evolving and its relationship to that symbol.[5] Christianity arrived at its symbols of universalism at a time when humanity required an image of spiritual unity that was independent of the sociopolitical myths of the empire and of the more localized myths of the tribes and the city-states. At the same time, the church, which stood to represent that new, universal order of humanity, was not completely able to clarify and actualize its character as its representative.[6] We still require compelling symbols for our unity as humans. Without such, the tensions between people erupt not only in political strife but also in increasingly bitter ideological and religious conflict. Some Christians have sought to find in themselves a reconciling vision fed by the spiritualities of these warring myths.[7]

Theologians who seek to work out a Christian perspective on religious pluralism that maintains the centrality of christology in their theological system find different ways of relating Christ to a transcultural process. Some begin with Teilhard de Chardin's observation that life in the universe tends toward greater complexity. This same complexity fosters higher levels of unity, which finally manifests itself in consciousness.[8] The diversity of religious traditions should also foster such a new unity. Humanity must be pushed beyond its provincialism in the religious sphere, so that each tradition both maintains its own integrity and enriches itself in the dialogue with other traditions.[9] Christians must acknowledge that the "transculturalization" of Christ means that Christianity does not have explicit revelation of religious reality which is only partial or implicit in other traditions. Real dialogue implies that Christians, too, learn authentic values that are either underexpressed or not expressed at all in their own tradition.[10] Perhaps the Christian will come face-to-face with the hidden Christ and learn to know him again for the first time.[11]

The drive toward new, unifying images cannot come only from Christian theologians. The conflicts and separations that divide the globe show us that we need an image of human unity before the divine, which will mobilize human beings to act on behalf of all the earth. The global appeal of Marxism's secular ideology discloses the void left by insufficient religious symbolization.[12] Entry into such a global dialogue may be even more difficult for other religious traditions than for Christianity, which has had some experience with deculturalization.[13] Here too, the Christian can learn something from God's own self-emptying (*kenosis*) on the cross. The God revealed in Jesus is not and never was a God of domination. Rather than a "moral rearmament," Christians might find themselves called to a "spiritual disarmament." Stripped of the trappings of imperialism, Christianity may find itself as a universal servant. Called to witness to Christ as a revelation of God's own *pathos* in history, "the Christian trusts that the *pathos* is itself more completely mediated to the world. Yet it is a witness that recognizes its limited, albeit necessary, role under God's sovereignty in history."[14]

Witnessing to a Transcultural Christ

Any founder of a world religion might be said to call people to an authentic humanity. Any one founder might be said to have had universal significance. Many Christians suspect that a transcultural Christ will mean a Christ who is one among many human religious founders. Christianity has a particular subject matter about which to speak, however. It does not begin with the fortuitous accidents of Jesus' personality or the sociopolitical realities through which he lived out his life. Rather, it begins with the identification of Jesus with God's cause. Jesus' life and fate engage us in an ethical critique of human suffering. They insist that we view history and our human obligations from the side of those who suffer, not from the side of those who have power.[15] At the same time, the message of reconciliation is addressed to all. The gospel is not the advocate for the sinner or the oppressed to the exclusion of the righteous or the wealthy.[16] Similarly, a transcultural christology cannot be the advocate for Christians to the exclusion of others from its vision. Statements about "ultimacy" cannot be centered exclusively in the image of Jesus. They must take into account the whole story of God, creation, and humanity. Beginning with the biblical witness, they may also speak about God from other religious traditions. The God about whom Jesus speaks and whom he incarnates is not some unknown, suddenly appearing in the world for the first time. He is the one who "has been from the beginning."

Five models are used by different theologians to express the universality of Christ in relationship to humanity as a whole. Although all may be criticized for being too narrowly limited to concerns of twentieth-century Western Christians, they represent attempts to embrace the larger experience of humanity.

Cosmological model. For those who build on the thought of Teilhard de Chardin, the resurrection prefigures the goal of the evolutionary process, a transfiguration of spirit-matter.[17] This goal, however, is not to be conceived as the termination of a strict chain of material causes. Evolution's move into consciousness has introduced a radical new contingency: human freedom. Humanity may fail to realize its destiny and wipe the entire species from the face of the earth. Christians should never be tempted to think that Christ's victory in the resurrection guarantees human freedom against such disasters. If anything, Christians are called toward a greater responsibility to creation than before. They must witness to God's caring through the Spirit active in the world and to human responsibility for creation.

Anthropological model. We recognize that human freedom and self-transcendence have an opening toward God that is extremely fragile. Humans may easily fail to acknowledge that openness. They may even suspect, on the basis of their experiences of failure and of incompleteness, that humans cannot commit themselves to others with the unreserved love of the other and desire for the other's well-being that has been the ideal of humanity. Psychoanalytic theories even proclaim such love to be an illusion.[18] A realist christology, which begins from the anthropological model, rejects those theories about the adequacy of the creature to God. That question has been answered in the incarnation, in God's own self-emptying.[19] The anthropological question is seen to be at its root a question about how we can commit ourselves to lives that are unreservedly dedicated to the love of neighbor. That commitment is grounded in the promise of God's future, the conviction that death is not the final word on human life. The suffering of the righteous is not sealed up in the past—a miserable page of human history.[20]

Eschatological model. Salvation is mediated in the story of God's justice confronting people in the concrete situations of their lives. The prophets who pronounced Yahweh's judgment on the nations also provide an opening for seeing the same justice at stake outside the confines of Yahwism. God's own deity is at stake in the crucifixion. Jesus' identification with the kingdom made his fate representative of God's faithfulness and integrity in the world. The cross reveals that in an alienated world the presence and rule of God can only take the shape of the Crucified One. The resurrection promises that the cross is not in vain. By pointing toward the identification of Jesus with God's cause even more clearly than the preaching of Jesus had done, the resurrection also presses the question "why" even more urgently. Why does the one who is righteous beyond all others suffer and die? How is humanity implicated in his death? What future "opens out" from the resurrection for such a humanity?[21]

Liberation model. Liberation models are the most common subset of eschatological models. Northern European and American liberation theologians stress the theoretical side of liberation as the true hermeneutic of the gospel. South Americans, on the other hand, seek to interpret Jesus out of the direct experience of struggle for liberation.[22] The struggle for liberation cannot begin until it is seen to be God's project, and not the projection of another human ideology. The weakness of identification with the oppressed, the poor, and the outcast might seem insurmountable without the assurance of the cross and the resurrection that it is God's own cause.

Psychological model. We have seen that the image of Jesus as a fully realized human person is the basis for a number of psychological models of his significance. Cast in individualistic terms, such models are always open to the charge of being part of the twentieth-century Western preoccupation with protecting and fulfilling the individual ego,[23] but models can be formulated which are neither individualistic nor aimed at "ego protection." Those who turn to the Adam images in the New Testament see Christianity as looking beyond the renewal of Israel to the renewal of humanity itself as what God intended.[24] Freedom from sin exhibited in Jesus means freedom from all the tendencies toward negation and despair which eat at human lives and destroy the relationships between humans. Jesus' total and unimpeded intimacy with God means that the will of God is not experienced as external, as commandment, as stern fate. The will of God is genuine fulfillment. Jesus' freedom from ego projections and guilt makes it possible to be open to others without the projections and entanglements that mar our human relationships. Others are free in the presence of such a person, since they are not trapped in the complex web of ego needs, expectations, and manipulation. This freedom must be expressed in the formation of new patterns of human relationship, a new fellowship. Such a fellowship also requires its foundation in a new revelation about God, since God is no longer the projection of all the deep suspicions of the human psyche. God is not the one who "holds all the cards" over against a humanity whose envy and hostility surface in archaic stories of the murder of the father.[25] This model sees Christ summoning humanity to another self, not to the ego-oriented ideals of autonomy and independence that have been the project of the West since the Enlightenment and seem to be exported along with our technology into the rest of the world.[26]

Each model seeks a point of entry into the larger questions of salvation and human destiny that face people today. Each acknowledges the radically unfinished character of the story of humanity. God continues to be involved in the story of the peoples of the world in such a way that no single culture can claim a monopoly on the processes of reconciliation and integration. God's involvement in history as we see it imaged in the Bible also suggests that there is no "pure essence" of salvation, which might be distilled from the religious experiences of humanity.[27] The transcultural Christ exists in and through the varied cultural forms that religions take in the world, but Christ is never limited to or identified with the particular historical standpoint of Christians. Thus the question about Jesus remains unfinished.

Summary

Christianity has always been committed to a universalism that finds in Jesus God's salvation for humanity as a whole. In the twentieth century, Christians cannot maintain that conviction without recognizing that other religious traditions also reveal God. Their expressions of faith in the ultimacy or universality of Christ must permit constructive and serious dialogue with the rest of humanity. This dialogue is grounded in the unity of the God who is revealed in Jesus and in other traditions. Yet we cannot know fully what those traditions reveal to us about God until that dialogue advances out of scholars' studies into the shared experience of humanity. The Bible provides some aids to Christians as they seek a position beyond the "christomonism" of an inbred theology. It looks to the larger question of God's faithfulness to creation. It sees Jesus' messianic office as God's response to the contingencies of sin and righteousness of a particular people at a particular time.

Yet the particular response in Jesus has a universalism that spreads out from that situation to all humanity. God's faithfulness may be mediated to humanity in other ways as well. If God is indeed Jesuslike, however, God will always be found on the side of the weak. Human freedom will not be created and grounded in the divine if it embodies the dynamics of power and conflict. Indeed, a unifying image of God beyond conflict, exclusiveness, and domination seems to be one of the major needs of humanity.

Some theologians seek to find this new vision in a transcultural Christ. Cosmological, anthropological, eschatological, liberation, and psychological models have all been called into play to show the relevance of Christ to all humanity. At the same time, such a genuinely transcultural image cannot be created by Christians alone. Each of the five models has a certain human contingency. Each is a point of entry into the human quest for salvation which remains unfinished. The cosmological model uses the resurrection to prefigure the next step in the transformation of spirit-matter. The anthropological model sees Christ as the realization of our human potential for openness and love toward our neighbor. The eschatological model reminds us that what is at stake in human history is no less than God's justice, a justice that confronts people in their concrete circumstances as both promise and judgment. The liberation model sees the identification of God's cause with the weak and suffering as the fundamental imperative for action. The norm is the imperative derived from the perspective of the weak. Finally, the psychological model presents an intimacy with God and humans that is possible only if the ego project of post-Enlightenment humanity is fundamentally changed. Control and autonomy are not the most important norms for selfhood. Consequently there is room for other selves and cultures beside those so dear to Western society.

Clearly, the resources of our religious traditions are being challenged as never before. Yet the challenge should not be cause for alarm. Christianity began by expanding the symbolic resources of one tradition with those of others, as it responded to a new experience of God's presence. Surely the religious traditions of the world have resources enough and more to meet the present crises of human history if they can be given voice. If we can venture out to explore the unknown reaches of space, we can certainly be as venturesome in the religious sphere. The conviction that the central insight of Christianity acknowledges God's presence in Jesus implies that the "unknown" Christ continually waits to be discovered.

FOR FURTHER READING

Smith, W. C. *Towards a World Theology*. Philadelphia: Westminster Press, 1981. An important assessment of the problem of giving an adequate theological assessment of world religions. Smith suggests that recovery of the foundational category "faith" may provide a perspective from which one can integrate a pluralistic, global religious understanding.

Rahner, K. "Jesus Christ in the Non-Christian Religions." *Theological Investigations*, vol. 17, pp. 39–50. New York: Crossroad, 1981. Rahner gives an a priori, dogmatic elaboration of principles that should govern the theologian's consideration of the problem of world religions. Since Christianity has not been influenced by the culture in which the other world religions developed, the traditions on which a theologian might draw do not have data that would answer questions about the mediation of salvation in other religious traditions. However, the saving presence of God, through the Spirit, must be made available to humans in those traditions. Since Christ is the "final cause" of God's saving action through the Spirit, the expectation of ultimate salvation in those traditions must also be related to the salvation Christians have found in Christ.

Davis, C. *Theology and Political Society*. New York and Cambridge: Cambridge University Press, 1980. An excellent introduction to the problems and diversity of political theology. Davis draws careful distinctions between the South American liberation theologians and the "political theology" that has developed from a more theoretical concern for praxis among North American and European theologians.

King, U. *Towards a New Mysticism: Teilhard de Chardin and Eastern Religions*. New York: Seabury Press, 1980. King applies a Teilhardian perspective to the development of religions. She suggests that their diversity should be brought under the unifying perspective of mysticism.

Thompson, W. *Jesus, Lord and Savior: A Theopathic Christology and Soteriology*. New York: Paulist Press, 1980. Pages 250–76. Thompson presents the argument for development of a "transcultural Christ" based on the work of Thomas Merton and Raimundo Panikkar.

Other theologians argue that "ultimacy of Christ" suggests an unwarranted Christocentric perspective. Christians should recover the genuine monotheism of their faith. Then the encounter with other religions will be mediated through the centrality of God, not Jesus. See especially the following works:

Milet, J. *God or Christ: The Excesses of Christocentricity*. New York: Crossroad, 1981. Milet traces the history of christology in the Roman Catholic tradition. He argues against a corruption of piety which places Jesus rather than God in the center of the believer's life.

TeSelle, E. *Christ in Context: Divine Purpose and Human Possibility*. Philadelphia: Fortress Press, 1975. TeSelle traces the retreat into Christocentricity of Protestant theology in the modern period. He argues that this retreat simply surrendered large portions of the world, human experience, and the biblical tradition. Consequently Christocentrism and christology became the area theologians felt was their territory, and theology became dangerously unbalanced and out of contact with the rest of human life.

NOTES

1. See J. A. T. Robinson, *Truth Is Two-Eyed* (Philadelphia: Westminster Press, 1979), pp. 41–100.

2. P. Ricoeur, *The Symbolism of Evil* (Boston: Beacon Press, 1967), pp. 3–18. See the extended discussion of the need for a world theology in W. C. Smith, *Towards a World Theology* (Philadelphia: Westminster Press, 1981), pp. 130–79. Smith insists that we cannot begin the necessary dialogue without recognizing our common religious history. He argues that christology will be displaced from the center to make way for a genuinely theocentric theology. Smith objects to the christologies that speak of a once-for-all revelation or salvation associated with the historical Jesus. The religious issue is not, he insists, what God did in the past but what he will do in the present and future, the living experience of believers (pp. 175–77).

3. E. TeSelle, *Christ in Context: Divine Purpose and Human Possibility* (Philadelphia: Fortress Press, 1975), pp. 131–63.

4. See Smith, *Towards a World Theology*, pp. 110–12, against the idea that there can be a Christian theology of religions.

5. Ibid., pp. 154–56. Smith questions the theory of history which supposes that the recovery of the origins of religion means the recovery of its truth.

6. See E. Voeglin, *Order in History IV: The Ecumenic Age* (Baton Rouge: Louisiana State University Press, 1974), pp. 134–37.

7. On the quest for the transcultural Christ in Thomas Merton and Raimundo Panikkar, see W. Thompson, *Jesus, Lord and Savior: A Theopathic Christology and Soteriology* (New York: Paulist Press, 1980), pp. 250–76. Smith, *Towards a World Theology*, pp. 152–79, sees a possible theistic renewal by recovering the fundamental category of faith.

8. G. Martelet, *The Risen Christ and the Eucharistic World* (New York: Seabury Press; London: William Collins & Co., 1976), pp. 51–53. Christ is the "supreme mutant" (p. 84).

9. E.g., P. Berger, *The Heretical Imperative* (New York: Doubleday & Co., 1979), pp. 157–89.

10. Thompson, *Jesus, Lord and Savior*, p. 268. Such learning need not imply that Christian theology will take all the concepts from its dialogue with the other traditions in the same sense given to them by adherents of those traditions.

11. E.g., see the use of Indian categories to illuminate the mystery of the Trinity in R. Panikkar, *The Trinity and World Religions* (Madras: Christian Literature Society, 1970).

12. J. Metz, *Faith in History and Society* (New York: Seabury Press, 1980), pp. 67–76.

13. Nor will the difficulties all be found in the same place or even on the same level from one tradition to another. See the illuminating "thought experiment" in interreligious dialogue conducted by Smith, *Towards a World Theology*, pp. 131–50.

14. Thompson, *Jesus, Lord and Savior*, p. 271.

15. See E. Schillebeeckx, *Jesus: An Experiment in Christology* (New York: Seabury Press, 1979), pp. 597–625.

16. People often concentrate on Jesus' message to sinners and forget his efforts to call the righteous to the same unifying vision of God's rule. See P. Perkins, *Hearing the Parables of Jesus* (New York: Paulist Press, 1981), pp. 53–62.

17. Martelet, *Risen Christ*, p. 84; and the application of the evolutionary model to dialogue with the mystic traditions of other religions in U. King, *Towards a New Mysticism: Teilhard de Chardin and Eastern Religions* (New York: Seabury Press, 1980), pp. 167–91.

18. See the rejection of the love commandment in S. Freud, *Civilization and Its Discontents* (New York: W.W. Norton, 1961), pp. 55–63.

19. See K. Rahner, "On the Theology of the Incarnation," *Theological Investigations*, vol. 4 (New York: Seabury Press, 1966), pp. 105–17.

20. See K. Rahner, "The Quest for Approaches Leading to an Understanding of the Mystery of the God-Man Jesus," *Theological Investigations*, vol. 13 (New York: Seabury Press, 1975), pp. 199–200.

21. J. Moltmann, *The Crucified God* (New York: Harper & Row, 1974), pp. 145–93.

22. See the discussion of liberation theologies in C. Davis, *Theology and Political Society* (New York and Cambridge: Cambridge University Press, 1980), pp. 14–27.

23. Even the modern preoccupation with spiritual journey seems designed to protect believers rather than expose them to the unfinished danger and the real pain of exodus; see M. Marty, *The Public Church* (New York: Crossroad, 1981), pp. 33–43.

24. On the corporate nature of New Testament christological terms, see C. F. D. Moule, *The Origin of Christology* (New York and Cambridge: Cambridge University Press, 1977), pp. 94–96.

25. See the discussion of archaism in Freud's interpretation of God in P. Ricoeur, *Freud and Philosophy* (New Haven, Conn.: Yale University Press, 1970), pp. 535–49.

26. See Schillebeeckx, *Jesus*, pp. 607–38; Thompson, *Jesus, Lord and Savior*, pp. 184–85.

27. Smith, *Towards a World Theology*, pp. 191–92.

Index of Biblical References

Old Testament

Apocrypha/Deutero-Canonical

New Testament

Index of Subjects